For those grand ladies who walked here before us, who with wisdom

and dedication began the efforts to preserve our building,

and for those who continue that effort today…

especially those who graciously shared

their "secrets" to make this book

a reality

PREFACE

This small book combines vignettes of the charmed life in Tampa

at the turn of the century with fine recipes only now being shared by some

of the most accomplished Chiseler party givers, cooks and pastry makers.

Proceeds from the sale of *Victorian Secrets* will be used by the

Chiselers in their continuing work at Plant Hall, restoring and

preserving for all time one of the most captivating

Victorian icons in the United States.

ACKNOWLEDGMENTS

We offer deepest appreciation

To those who presented the inspiration for this volume

To Phyllis Kimbel for her ability to transport us through time with her delightful written word

To Charlie Greacen for his perceptive pen and ink drawings

To Melinda Chavez, Education Curator, Henry B. Plant Museum,

for the wealth of historical data she so graciously provided

To Gene McCall, Conservator, and Jan Abell, Architect,

for their assistance in researching the symbolism of the architectural ornamentation

and To ALL the good cooks whose recipes fill these pages!

CONTENTS

INTRODUCTION

Aging, out-of-style, silenced by the Depression, the fanciful old building stood vacant.

But even from across the river you could still feel its magic.

Had it not in its day been one of the world's grandest hotels? Its thirteen silver minarets,

cupolas and domes, tarnished though they were, shimmered enough in the Florida sun

to call up visions of an exotic land of turbaned, saber-flashing Moors.

And from back a ways, the lace-like trim on the verandas seemed pretty as ever.

By anyone's reckoning, the old Tampa Bay Hotel was a Victorian masterpiece.

The resort, built by railroad and steamship mogul Henry Bradley Plant,

was undoubtedly the jewel of the vast Plant empire. Fashionably modeled after the court of

Moorish kings in Granada, the quarter-mile-long hotel began to rise in the late 1800s

across the river from a sleepy little hamlet with cows and pigs wandering its streets.

Plant's hostelry had been designed by John A. Wood

of New York and appeared like a vision out of the *Arabian Nights*.

Yet it was solid built, the first reinforced concrete structure in the United States.

And it was fireproof, having been erected largely of obsolete narrow-gauge railroad track

and no less than 7,500 barrels of seashell. The hotel boasted total electrification

and plumbing; hot and cold water ran with but the turn of a faucet.

The entire brick-clad building was magnificently detailed in carved Cuban mahogany, double-thick French glass and pillars of pink granite. The finest art treasures that could be acquired by connoisseurs with unlimited funds and superb taste decorated the hotel's 511 rooms. Fresh bouquets from the conservatory blossomed everywhere and violin music floated through the corridors. It was a fairy-tale castle, a Victorian confection.

Only the nineteen-member faculty might have predicted that its fledgling private college, operating out of a high school gym, would someday become internationally known as an institute of academic excellence.

It was 1933 and the new University of Tampa had been searching for a suitable home. But money was frighteningly scarce. Armed with brooms and buckets, the staff moved into the abandoned, turreted resort hotel offered by the city. And in a remarkable show of selflessness and public spirit, all of the instructors agreed to teach for a year without pay.

Mattresses were hurriedly carried down the hall and piled to the ceiling as the second floor bedrooms of the old hotel were turned into classrooms.

The Victorian kitchen found new life as a chemistry lab and the resplendent dining
room was lined with library books. Ridding the building of rats, however, was
a slow process indeed. Nonetheless, lights soon were shining from the windows of the
palace-on-the river and the symbolism was not lost: both the struggling university
and the precious building were destined to survive and flourish.

The city's newly chartered museum settled into a first floor wing, gathering together what
remained of the priceless antique furniture and objects-of-art that the Plants, four
decades before, had brought back from Europe and the Orient. And so began the
Henry B. Plant Museum's laborious task of preserving and restoring with gentle care
Tampa's all but forgotten splendors; of capturing the fading memories, the
illusive allure of a bygone age; of holding dear a moment in time.

By 1959 the rest of the university building, now called Plant Hall, still carried scars

of neglect and abuse. In an effort to help erase some of the ravages of time, a

small group of women set about chiseling gray WPA paint off fireplace tiles. Their

chisels not only revealed beauty, but sparked a solemn commitment to save

the faded old pavilion whose glorious Victorian heart had nearly been stilled.

In its 38 years, The Chiselers, Inc. has grown into a nonprofit organization of 250 women

volunteers who have raised and utilized more than $1 million in the restoration of

the cornerstone of Tampa, a National Historic Landmark and proud symbol of its city.

This small book combines vignettes of the charmed life in Tampa at the turn

of the century with fine recipes only now being shared by some of the most

accomplished Chiseler party givers, cooks and pastry makers.

Proceeds from the sale of *Victorian Secrets* will be used by the Chiselers

in their continuing work at Plant Hall, restoring and preserving for all time

one of the most captivating Victorian icons in the United States.

APPETIZERS & BEVERAGES

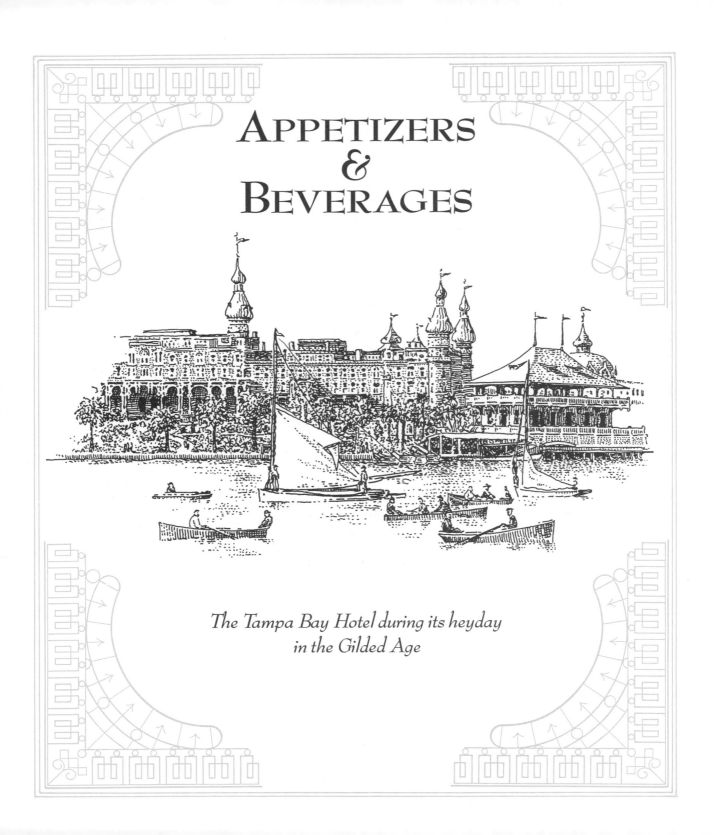

The Tampa Bay Hotel during its heyday
in the Gilded Age

How Fortunes Are Made
Henry B. Plant, 1819–1899

Henry Bradley Plant, a fatherless Connecticut lad,
began his illustrious career by quitting high school and signing on as a
deck hand. At the end of his life Plant owned one of the largest
conglomerates in America, a sprawling system of railroads, steamships,
express companies and hotels, which brought with it the delights of honor, fame
and fortune. But nothing would ever surpass the pleasure and satisfaction he felt when,
as an experienced deck hand/cabin boy, Henry was awarded the task of handling
Express packages on the coastal steamer. For now he could sleep in the ship's
comfortable mailroom and, for the first time in five years, no longer had to eat all his meals
standing up. Twenty years later, assisted by the unreliability of U.S. Postal shipping, Henry Plant
had not only expanded Adams Express, rival of Wells Fargo, all over the south but had also
become a southerner himself and, when the firm was reorganized as The Southern Express Company,
became its president. During the Civil War Jefferson Davis, hating "born Yankees,"
nonetheless entrusted Plant to handle all Confederacy shipments, including military
pay and confidential papers from General Robert E. Lee. After the surrender Plant
found himself in a position to buy up bankrupt southern railroads, combining them
into an efficient network by converting to standard-gauge rail. Plant
thereby put the town of Tampa on the map, connecting it by iron track
with the great cities of the northeast. His investment company brought
northern money south and eventually his vast holdings included
steamships. But Henry Plant's masterpiece, his monument, was the
fabled Tampa Bay Hotel, a palatial showcase for the social
magnificence of the Gilded Age.

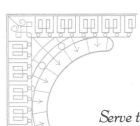

CAPONATA

Serve the caponata with salami, black olives, anchovies, mozzarella cheese cubes and other favorite additions for a mixed antipasto. Or combine the caponata with tuna and French bread for a light summer supper.

1 eggplant	1/2 cup chopped fresh parsley
1/2 cup olive oil	2 tablespoons dried basil
1 red bell pepper	1/4 cup red wine vinegar
2 (14-ounce) cans Italian tomatoes	2 tablespoons tomato paste
1/2 cup pimento-stuffed olives	1 1/2 tablespoons sugar
1 1/2 cups chopped celery	1 tablespoon salt, or to taste
2 cloves of garlic, sliced	1 teaspoon coarsely ground pepper

Rinse the eggplant and pat dry. Cut the unpeeled eggplant into cubes smaller than an inch. Heat the olive oil in a large skillet. Add the eggplant and sauté briefly. Cut the red pepper into bite-size pieces. Drain the tomatoes and cut into pieces. Cut the olives into halves if they are large. Add the red pepper, tomatoes, olives, celery, garlic, parsley, basil, vinegar, tomato paste, sugar, salt and pepper to the skillet and stir gently and carefully until mixed. Reduce the heat to a simmer and cook, covered, for 30 minutes. Drain the vegetables, reserving the liquid. Cook the reserved liquid until reduced to a thick consistency. Add the reduced liquid to the eggplant mixture and mix gently to avoid breaking the vegetables. Chill until serving time.

Yield: 6 servings

Phyllis Kimbel

Escargot with Wild Mushrooms

1 (24-ounce) can escargot
1 shallot, finely chopped
6 ounces mixed wild mushrooms
2 tablespoons butter
¼ ounce brandy

Salt and white pepper to taste
6 ounces demi-glace
4 ounces bleu cheese
15 to 20 miniature thin
pastry cups

Rinse the escargot and drain well. Sauté the escargot, shallot and mushrooms in butter in a sauté pan. Remove the mixture to a bowl. Deglaze the pan with brandy. Add the salt, pepper, demi-glace and crumbled bleu cheese. Add to the snails and mix well. Spoon into the pastry cups.
Note: If using dried mushrooms, prepare by soaking according to the package directions. If demi-glace is not available, use beef bouillon that has been reduced by ½.

Yield: 15 to 20 servings

Kathryn Turner

Bead-and-Reel Design

The bead-and-reel design runs across the lintel of the hotel's grand entry doorway. Like a weaver's woof, which winds its way back and forth through the weft, it symbolizes the Thread of Life, at once both strong and tenuous.

Appetizers & Beverages

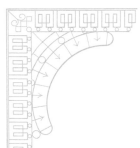

MARINATED SHRIMP

1 clove of garlic	3/4 teaspoon salt
2 pounds cooked shrimp	3 tablespoons lemon juice
1/2 cup chopped celery	1/4 teaspoon Tabasco sauce
1 scallion, chopped	2 tablespoons chili sauce
1 tablespoon chopped chives	2 tablespoons catsup
6 tablespoons olive oil	2 tablespoons horseradish
1/4 teaspoon paprika	1 tablespoon prepared mustard

Rub a large bowl with the garlic. Peel and devein the shrimp and pat dry. Place the shrimp in the prepared bowl. Combine the scallion, chives, olive oil, paprika, salt, lemon juice, Tabasco sauce, chili sauce, catsup, horseradish and mustard in a bowl and mix well. Pour over the shrimp and mix gently until coated. Marinate, covered, in the refrigerator for 6 to 12 hours. Drain well and mound on an hors d'oeuvre platter. Serve with wooden picks.

Yield: 10 to 12 servings

Mary Jean Gibson

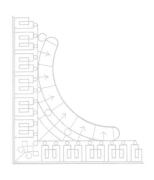

Cinnie's Cheese Puffs

1 (1-pound) loaf unsliced white bread	4 ounces sharp cheese, shredded
½ cup butter	2 egg whites
3 ounces cream cheese	

Remove the crusts on all sides of the bread loaf. Cut the bread into 1-inch cubes. Combine the butter, cream cheese and sharp cheese in the top of a double boiler. Heat over hot water until the butter and cheeses melt and are well blended, stirring frequently. Remove from the heat. Beat the egg whites in a bowl until stiff peaks form. Fold the egg whites into the cheese mixture gently; the mixture will be lumpy. Dip the bread cubes into the mixture, coating well. Arrange the coated cubes on a baking sheet; do not allow the cubes to touch. Freeze for 2 hours or longer. Place the frozen cubes in sealable plastic bags. Store in the freezer. Remove from the freezer and arrange on baking sheets. Bake at 400 degrees for 20 minutes or until golden brown.

Yield: 6 dozen

Lynne Smith

Not to be Trifled With

Tampa had never figured in Henry Plant's original scheme. When it was learned that Plant needed to purchase only one more property before establishing his railroad terminus in their town, the folks of Cedar Key quickly upped the price. They obviously did not know Henry Bradley Plant. Angered, he swore to wipe Cedar Key off the map. "Owls will hoot in your attics and hogs will wallow in your streets!" he warned. And with that Plant tore up his plans for Cedar Key and headed out to another little burg called Tampa.

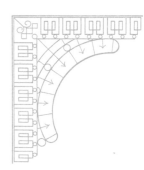

GOAT CHEESE TART

1 unbaked pie pastry
Roasted red peppers
2 to 3 shallots
9 to 11 ounces goat cheese
1 clove of garlic

¼ cup fresh dill
1 cup heavy cream
3 eggs
White pepper to taste

Fit the pie pastry into a quiche or tart pan. Arrange a layer of the roasted peppers
in the pie shell. Combine the shallots, goat cheese, garlic, dill, cream, eggs and pepper in a blender
or food processor and purée the mixture. Fill the pie shell to ½ inch from the top.
(Pour any remaining filling into a small loaf pan and bake with the tart for a cook's treat.)
Bake at 350 degrees for 45 minutes or until puffed and golden brown.
Serve the tart warm or at room temperature.

Yield: 8 servings

Sherrill O'Neal

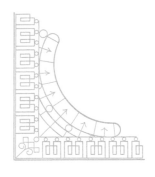

CHEESE AND CRAB MEAT PUFFS

1 (5-ounce) jar Old English cheese
spread, softened
1/2 cup butter, softened
1 (6-ounce) can crab meat,
drained, flaked

1/4 teaspoon salt
1/4 teaspoon garlic powder
1 tablespoon mayonnaise
6 English muffins, split

Blend the cheese spread and butter in a bowl. Stir in the next 4 ingredients. Spread the crab meat mixture on the muffin halves. Cut each into fourths and arrange on a baking sheet. Freeze until firm. Place the frozen pieces in sealable plastic bags. Store in the freezer. Remove from the freezer and arrange on a baking sheet. Bake at 400 degrees for 10 minutes or until light brown.

Yield: 4 dozen

Lorraine Miller

CUCUMBER TOAST POINTS

6 slices white bread
1 teaspoon lemon juice
1/2 cup mayonnaise
1/2 teaspoon curry powder

1 cucumber, peeled
Parmesan cheese to taste
Parsley flakes to taste
Paprika to taste

Trim the crusts from the bread. Cut the slices diagonally to make triangles. Mix the lemon juice, mayonnaise and curry powder in a bowl. Spread the mixture on the bread triangles to the edges. Slice the cucumber 1/4 inch thick. Place a cucumber slice on each triangle. Sprinkle with the remaining ingredients. Place on a baking sheet and broil until light brown.

Yield: 12 servings

Marsha Dickey

Spinach Sandwiches

1 (10-ounce) package frozen
chopped spinach, thawed
3 green onions, finely chopped
1/2 (8-ounce) can water chestnuts,
chopped
2 tablespoons mayonnaise

1/2 teaspoon salt
1/2 teaspoon cayenne
1/2 teaspoon garlic salt
Worcestershire sauce to taste
Thinly sliced bread

Drain the spinach very well. Combine with the green onions, water chestnuts, mayonnaise, salt, cayenne, garlic salt and Worcestershire sauce in a bowl and mix well. Spread on half the bread slices and top with the remaining slices. Trim the crusts from the sandwiches and cut into squares or triangles.

Yield: variable

Josephine Pizzo, Widow of Tampa Historian Tony Pizzo

Vision

The townfolk who had not succumbed to yellow fever had literally run for their lives. Businesses were closing down. Tampa was finished. But Henry Plant had a knack for seeing into the future and he arrived on the scene a bearer of hope, promising to spend millions of dollars in the dispirited village. His first undertaking was to build one of the world's finest ports and lay railroad lines out to it and his new Inn, after which he broke ground for construction of the grandiose Tampa Bay Hotel. Overnight, Tampa turned into a boom town.

VIDALIA ONION DIP

2 cups minced Vidalia onion
2 cups shredded Swiss cheese
1 1/2 cups mayonnaise

1 teaspoon celery salt
1 teaspoon dillweed
1/4 teaspoon white pepper

Combine the onion, cheese, mayonnaise, celery salt, dillweed and white pepper in a bowl and mix well. Spoon the mixture into a 2-quart casserole. Bake at 350 degrees for 30 minutes or until brown and bubbly. Serve hot with favorite crackers, chips or crudites.

Yield: 5 to 6 cups

Cookie Bailey

DURANGO DIP

1 pound sausage
16 ounces cream cheese

1 (10-ounce) can tomatoes
with green chiles

Cook the sausage in a skillet until brown and crumbly, stirring frequently; drain well. Melt the cream cheese in a saucepan over low heat, stirring constantly. Drain the tomatoes with green chiles, reserving the liquid. Add the tomatoes to the cream cheese and mix well. Stir in the sausage and enough of the reserved tomato liquid to make the dip of the desired consistency. Heat to serving temperature. Serve with tortilla or nacho chips.

Yield: 5 cups

Wilma Martin

Fabulous Hot Shrimp Dip

This dip was served by the old Tampa Bay Art Center for one of their affairs and was such a hit that it was featured in the newspaper the following week.

8 ounces cream cheese
1/3 cup mayonnaise
1 (6-ounce) can shrimp
1 tablespoon minced onion

1 teaspoon Worcestershire sauce
Sherry to taste
Salt and pepper to taste

Heat the cream cheese in a saucepan over very low heat just until melted, stirring constantly. Remove from the heat and blend in the mayonnaise. Drain the shrimp and chop into pieces. Add the shrimp, onion, Worcestershire sauce, sherry, salt and pepper to the cream cheese mixture and mix well. Spoon into a chafing dish to keep warm. Serve with corn chips or tortilla chips. This dip can be made in large quantities for parties and will keep well in the refrigerator for several days.
Variation: Substitute fresh shrimp for the canned shrimp.
Yield: 4 to 6 servings

Mia Hardcastle

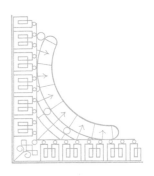

Baked Brie

1 (10-ounce) round Brie cheese
¼ cup chopped parsley
1 clove of garlic, mashed
2 tablespoons minced red bell pepper
1 tablespoon minced chives
2 ounces pepperoni, chopped

¼ cup chopped mushrooms
1 teaspoon oregano
1 egg
1 tablespoon water
1 sheet frozen puff pastry, thawed

Freeze the Brie for 30 minutes. Combine the parsley, garlic, red pepper, chives, pepperoni, mushrooms and oregano in a bowl and mix well. Slice the Brie horizontally into 2 layers. Spread the pepperoni mixture on the bottom layer and replace the top layer, pressing together firmly. Beat the egg with water to make an egg glaze. Roll the puff pastry to a 12-inch square on a lightly floured surface. Place the Brie in the center. Fold the pastry to the center of the Brie, brush the edges with the egg glaze and press together to seal. Turn the wrapped Brie over and brush on all sides with the egg glaze. Let stand for 5 minutes to dry. Cut 5 or 6 slits on the top. Wrap the Brie tightly. Store in the freezer. Remove from the freezer and thaw for 1½ hours at room temperature. Unwrap the Brie and place in an ungreased pie plate or quiche pan. Bake at 400 degrees for 30 minutes or until the pastry is golden brown and puffed. Cool for 15 minutes before serving.

Yield: variable

Pat Gillen

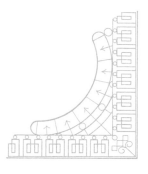

Pâté de Foie Gras

*This is easy to do while preparing your Christmas goose for the oven, but try
it anytime substituting chicken livers—no one will know.*

1 goose liver	½ teaspoon salt
1 piece of onion	⅛ teaspoon nutmeg
1 celery top	1 teaspoon hot English mustard
Salt to taste	1 teaspoon finely grated onion
Cayenne to taste	Generous pinch of ground cloves
½ cup butter	

Combine the goose liver, onion piece and celery top in a saucepan. Add water to cover
and salt and cayenne to taste. Simmer for about 15 minutes or until the liver is tender. Remove
the liver and press through a sieve while still warm. The amount of sieved liver should
be about ½ cup. Add the butter, ½ teaspoon salt, nutmeg, mustard, grated onion
and cloves and mix well. Pack the mixture into a small crock and chill, covered, until
serving time. Serve the pâté with plain melba toast.

Yield: 4 servings

Phyllis Kimbel

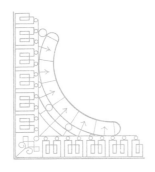

Zesty North Carolina Pot Cheese

2 pounds Velveeta cheese
1 cup margarine
8 ounces French onion dip

1 cup Catalina salad dressing
1 (5-ounce) bottle cream-style
horseradish

Cut the cheese into pieces and place in the top of a large double boiler over simmering water.
Add the margarine, onion dip, salad dressing and horseradish. Heat until the ingredients
are melted and well mixed, stirring frequently. Pour the mixture about ⅓ at a time into a
blender and process until smooth. Pour into 6-ounce jelly or canning jars and cover
with the lids. Store in the refrigerator for up to 6 months.

Yield: 5 jars or more

Martha Turner

All Aboard!

*Even at the end of the 19th century there were those who had never
heard the roar, the clang, the hoot and huff of a railroad train, nor felt the
majesty of machines thundering over rails. As Henry Plant's
iron horse chugged into Tampa in a cloud of blue smoke, folks stood in
awe of its engineering, of its romance —when suddenly the whistle blew,
causing great fright to the women!*

CAFÉ BRÛLOT FOR FOUR

This recipe was given to Dr. C. Frank Chunn by Louis at Arnaud's in New Orleans where it is served with the lights dimmed and a great flourish. Dr. Chunn used a copper and alloy Brûlot bowl with a strainer ladle and had considerable success except for the time he was ladling from so great a height that the flaming mixture spilled over and took the finish off the table.

4 lumps of sugar
4 cinnamon sticks
4 pinches whole cloves
Thin strips of lemon and orange peel

6 ounces brandy
2 inches vanilla bean
4 demitasse cups double-strength
hot coffee

Combine the first 6 ingredients in a metal (not silver) bowl. Ignite the brandy and dim the lights; let the flame subside. Ladle the ingredients together for 20 to 30 seconds. Add the hot coffee and ladle the mixture into the cups. The second batch is even better than the first.

Yield: 4 servings

Marjorie Chunn Cochran, Charter Member

THE WHISPER

1 large scoop coffee ice cream
1 tablespoon brandy

1 tablespoon dark creme de cacao

Process the ice cream, brandy and creme de cacao in a blender for a second or two or just until blended. Pour into a 4- to 5-ounce parfait glass and serve with a straw.

Yield: 1 serving

Jane Watson

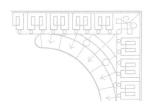

Mauricio's Sangria

²/₃ bottle Spanish red wine
3 ounces good Spanish brandy
(such as El Presidente)
Dash of Triple Sec or other
orange liqueur

¼ cup sugar
Orange and apple slices
Ice cubes and seltzer water
to taste

Combine the wine, brandy, Triple Sec, sugar and fruit slices in a large pitcher. Refrigerate for several hours. Add the desired amounts of ice cubes and seltzer water just before serving.

Yield: variable

Sarah Jane Rubio

July 26, 1888

Every shop in town closed for the day. The cornerstone of the new hotel was about to be laid by the Mayor with Henry Plant himself looking on, three leading citizens were clearing their throats in readiness to display powers of oratory, a photographer was crouched under his camera cover and the band leader had just begun to wave his baton. Nothing so grand had ever occurred in Tampa and more than 200 people had crossed the river to watch and to dream.

Faux White Sangria Punch

*This delicious, refreshing nonalcoholic punch was served for
many years at the Henry B. Plant birthday parties on the East Veranda.
The recipe is shared by Carlino Catering.*

1 Fruited Ice Ring
1 large bottle unsweetened white
grape juice, chilled
1 (or more) lemon
1 (or more) lime

1 (or more) orange
Dash of cinnamon
2 (1-liter) bottles diet ginger
ale, chilled

Place the ice ring in a punch bowl. Add the grape juice. Slice the lemon, lime and orange
into thin slices. Cut each slice into fourths and add to the punch bowl. Add a dash
of cinnamon. Add the ginger ale just as the guests are arriving.

Yield: 35 servings

Fruited Ice Ring

Thin lemon slices
Thin lime slices

Thin orange slices

Select a large ice ring pan or gelatin mold. Pour enough water into the pan to cover the
bottom. Cut the citrus slices into pieces as desired and arrange a layer of the fruit in the pan.
Freeze until firm. Continue to add thin layers of water and fruit in the pan, freezing
each layer before adding the next. Store in the freezer until needed; the ice ring can be prepared
several days in advance. When ready to use, dip the bottom of the pan in warm water
and invert the ice ring into the punch bowl.

Yield: 1 ice ring

Patsy Woodroffe

Sherry Sour

1 (6-ounce) can frozen pink   1 fifth dry sherry
        lemonade, thawed

Combine the lemonade and sherry in a bowl and mix well. Pour into a freezer container.
Freeze for 1 day or longer for the best flavor; the mixture will not freeze solid but
will be slushy. Serve in cocktail glasses or punch cups.

Yield: 6 servings

Pat Martin

Fruited Iced Tea

2 tablespoons loose tea   1 cup orange juice
3 cups boiling water   3¾ cups cold water
²/₃ cup sugar
1 (6-ounce) can frozen lemonade
concentrate, thawed

Steep the tea in the boiling water in a teapot or covered container for 20 to 30 minutes.
Dissolve the sugar in the lemonade concentrate in a large pitcher. Strain the tea into the pitcher
and mix well. Stir in the orange juice and the cold water. Store in the refrigerator.

Yield: 2 quarts

Diane Kemker

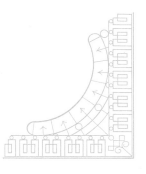

SALADS

*Guests view the hotel's
extensive gardens
by rickshaw.*

THE HAYDEN STORY

Back in the 1860s, Jesse Hayden had his eye on a fine parcel of land.
It lay just upriver from the fishing village and over the water from Fort Brooke.
Jesse was a good bargainer, but he still had to give both his white horse and wagon for the sixteen acres.
Twenty years later when Henry Plant was bringing the railroad down from the north and wanted
to build a hotel on the riverbank, it was Jesse's turn to hold the cards. Keeping his
homestead and a few acres of orange grove, Hayden shook hands with Plant's architect
over a figure of $40,000, each man highly pleased with the deal he had made.
Plant transformed his new property into a paradise neither Jesse nor the townsfolk could
have envisioned, by creating "the most luxurious hotel in the world" ensconced in a setting
to match the dream. Soon the subtropical acreage was laced with walkways curving
through exotic gardens, 150 species of trees, bushes, and flowers brought in from Europe
and the Caribbean. And gallant gentlemen were pulling their ladyloves through the sunny
winter gardens in rickshaws, or rowing them past these botanical glories in canoes upon the river.
But Jesse Hayden's boat was no longer plying the river. The tables had turned.
Honoring a promise it had made
with Henry Plant, Tampa Town
had thrown a sturdy bridge across
the Hillsborough River—
which put Jesse Hayden's ferry
squarely out of business.

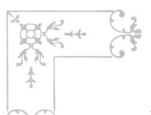

CREAMY APRICOT SALAD

2 (16-ounce) cans apricots
1 (20-ounce) can crushed pineapple
2 (3-ounce) packages apricot or
orange gelatin

1 envelope unflavored gelatin
2 tablespoons lemon juice
2 cups sour cream
1 cup chopped nuts

Drain the apricots and pineapple, reserving the juices. Add enough water to the reserved juices to measure 3 cups. Bring the juice mixture to a boil in a saucepan. Add the hot mixture to the gelatins in a large bowl and stir until the gelatin is completely dissolved. Mash the apricots and mix with the pineapple, lemon juice, sour cream and nuts. Add to the gelatin and mix well. Spray two 2-quart glass dishes lightly with nonstick cooking spray. Pour the gelatin mixture into the dishes. Chill until firm.

Yield: 12 to 20 servings

Sally Brorein

FLOWER-AND-TENDRIL DESIGN

In 1836 a prominent London architect traveled to Spain and began recording details of the Alhambra's architecture. Formalized plant shapes and curvilinear designs, such as the flower-and-tendril carved in the old lobby woodwork, typify the grace of Byzantine art and the eclecticism of Victorian style.

LEMON-LIME MOLD

1 (20-ounce) can crushed pineapple
1 (3-ounce) package lime gelatin
1 (3-ounce) package lemon gelatin
2 cups boiling water

8 ounces cream cheese, softened
1 cup chopped celery
1 cup chopped nuts
12 ounces whipped topping

Drain the pineapple, reserving the juice. Dissolve the gelatins in the boiling water
in a large bowl. Add the reserved pineapple juice. Chill the mixture until partially set. Combine
the pineapple, cream cheese, celery and nuts in a bowl and mix well. Add to the partially set
gelatin mixture. Fold in the whipped topping. Coat the inside of a large decorative gelatin mold
or bundt pan with mayonnaise. Spoon the gelatin mixture into the prepared mold.
Chill for 8 to 12 hours. Unmold the gelatin onto a serving platter.

Yield: 16 to 20 servings

Elaine Watson

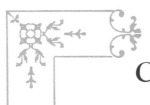

CONGEALED MINCEMEAT SALAD

1 (28-ounce) can sliced peaches
1 (20-ounce) can pineapple chunks
1 (3-ounce) package lemon gelatin
1 (3-ounce) package orange gelatin

1 cup mincemeat
3/4 to 1 cup ginger ale
1/2 to 1 cup pecans

Drain the fruit, reserving the juice. Cut the fruit into pieces and continue to drain.
Add enough water to the reserved juices to measure 2 cups. Bring the juice
mixture to a boil. Add to the gelatins in a large bowl and mix until completely dissolved.
Add the fruit and mincemeat and mix well. Let stand until cool. Add the ginger
ale and pecans. Pour into a 9x13-inch dish. Chill until firm.
Variation: Substitute 16-ounce cans of the peaches, pineapple and mincemeat and add a
can of apricots; omit the ginger ale and pecans and pour into individual gelatin molds.

Yield: 12 servings

Nell Rorebeck, Ann Thompson

THE INN

*A*s for convenience, it had everything. Henry Plant ran his railroad to the end
of a mile-long pier into the bay and there constructed the Port Tampa Inn.
Advertising pamphlets suggested guests might fish from their bedroom windows,
though the housekeeping staff, charged with cleaning the hardwood floors and
Persian rugs, must have wished otherwise. In spite of its attractiveness to fishermen,
the Inn was a pretty place of Queen Anne style with diamond-shaped
windowpanes and curry yellow-pine cabinetry. Afternoons, the
Tampa Bay Hotel orchestra journeyed over for concerts.

BROCCOLI AND APPLE SALAD

1 cup mayonnaise
2 tablespoons vinegar
2 teaspoons sugar
10 to 12 slices bacon
Florets of 2 bunches broccoli

1 medium red onion, chopped
3/4 cup raisins
1 apple, chopped
1 (11-ounce) can mandarin
    oranges, drained

Combine the mayonnaise, vinegar and sugar in a bowl and blend well. Set the dressing aside. Cook the bacon as desired until crisp. Drain on paper towels and set aside. Combine the broccoli florets, red onion, raisins and apple in a large bowl. Add the mayonnaise mixture to the broccoli mixture and toss until well mixed. Chill in the refrigerator for 2 to 3 hours or until ready to serve. Crumble the bacon. Add the bacon and mandarin oranges to the salad just before serving.

Yield: 12 servings

Patsy Woodroffe

Broccoli and Cashew Salad

6 slices bacon
Florets of 1 bunch broccoli
1 red onion, chopped
1/2 red bell pepper, chopped
1/2 cup raisins
3/4 cup roasted cashews

3/4 to 1 cup mayonnaise
1 tablespoon lemon juice
1 tablespoon sugar
1 teaspoon salt
1/2 teaspoon pepper

Fry the bacon in a skillet until crisp. Drain on paper towels, crumble and set aside. Combine the broccoli, onion, red pepper, raisins, cashews and bacon in a large bowl. Combine the mayonnaise, lemon juice, sugar, salt and pepper in a small bowl and blend well. Add to the broccoli mixture and toss until well mixed. Chill for several hours.

Yield: 6 servings

Carole Anderson

Cucumber Salad

2 cucumbers
1/2 cup sour cream
2 tablespoons lemon juice
1/4 cup vinegar

1/2 teaspoon salt
2 tablespoons sugar
Dash of red pepper

Cut the cucumbers into thin slices and place in a bowl. Combine the sour cream, lemon juice, vinegar, salt, sugar and red pepper in a small bowl and blend well. Pour over the cucumbers and mix gently to coat the cucumber slices. Chill for 2 hours or longer.

Yield: 6 servings

Beth Darr

Congealed Spinach Salad

A staple item at Maas Brothers Dining Room

1 (10-ounce) package frozen
chopped spinach, thawed
1 (3-ounce) package lemon gelatin
1 cup boiling water
1 cup mayonnaise

¹/₄ teaspoon wine vinegar
¹/₂ cup chopped fresh parsley
1 tablespoon minced onion
1 cup large curd cottage cheese

Drain the spinach and squeeze dry. Set the spinach aside. Dissolve the gelatin in boiling water in a bowl. Let stand until cool. Add the mayonnaise, vinegar, parsley and onion and mix well. Add the spinach and cottage cheese and mix well. Pour into a shallow dish. Chill until firm.

Yield: 8 to 10 servings

Pat Colvard

And They Lived Happily Ever After

*It was love at first sight. His eyes rested on her tender Irish beauty;
she was almost close enough to speak to, seated gracefully in the
New York City stagecoach. But with no one to introduce them....
Evening after evening he boarded the same stage and there she would be,
comely as ever. Henry Plant, widower, had fallen in love and he knew it.
Although he had as yet to speak his first word to her or know her name,
Henry boldly rapped on the door of her home and announced
to Margaret Loughman's startled parents that he wished to marry
their daughter! He was 55, the future Mrs. Plant just 25.*

STRAWBERRY AND STILTON SALAD

2 cups sliced strawberries
2 tablespoons chopped fresh basil
2 tablespoons raspberry vinegar
1/2 teaspoon sugar
1 teaspoon olive oil

1 teaspoon water
4 cups gourmet salad greens
1/4 cup crumbled Stilton or
feta cheese

Combine the strawberries, basil, raspberry vinegar and sugar in a bowl and toss until well mixed. Refrigerate, covered, for 1 hour. Strain the mixture, reserving the liquid. Set the strawberry mixture aside. Pour the reserved liquid into a small jar. Add the olive oil and water to the liquid, cover tightly and shake vigorously. Divide the greens among 4 salad plates. Add 1/2 cup strawberries, 2 teaspoons of the olive oil mixture and 1 tablespoon crumbled cheese to each plate. Serve with French bread.

Yield: 4 servings

Doris Harvey

RASPBERRY WALNUT SALAD

4 cups torn Boston lettuce
4 cups torn red leaf lettuce
³/4 cup chopped toasted walnuts
1 cup fresh raspberries

1 avocado, chopped
1 kiwifruit, peeled, sliced
2 green onions, chopped
Raspberry Salad Dressing

Combine the lettuces, walnuts, raspberries, avocado, kiwifruit and green onions in a large salad bowl and toss gently. Serve with the Raspberry Salad Dressing.

Yield: 12 servings

RASPBERRY SALAD DRESSING

¹/3 cup seedless raspberry jam
¹/3 cup raspberry vinegar
²/3 cup vegetable oil
1 teaspoon poppy seeds

1 teaspoon salt
¹/3 cup sugar
2 tablespoons lemon juice

Combine the jam, vinegar, oil, poppy seeds, salt, sugar and lemon juice in a blender container. Process until well mixed. Pour the dressing into a bowl or bottle. Chill, covered, until serving time.

Yield: 1¹/2 cups

Carole Anderson

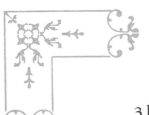

WALNUT STILTON SALAD

3 heads Boston Bibb lettuce	Vinaigrette Dressing
3/4 cup coarsely chopped walnuts	4 to 6 ounces Stilton cheese

Rinse the lettuce and dry well. Tear the lettuce into bite-size pieces and place in a large salad bowl. Add the walnuts and toss until well mixed. Add the Vinaigrette Dressing and toss to mix. Crumble the cheese and sprinkle over the top of the salad.

Yield: 8 servings

VINAIGRETTE DRESSING

1/4 cup red wine vinegar	1 tablespoon minced onion
3/4 cup olive oil	1 teaspoon dried basil
1 teaspoon Dijon mustard	1/2 teaspoon dried oregano
2 tablespoons water	1/2 teaspoon garlic powder
1 tablespoon chopped fresh parsley	Salt and pepper to taste

Combine the vinegar, olive oil, mustard and water in a jar. Add the parsley, onion, basil, oregano, garlic powder, salt and pepper and shake vigorously to mix. Chill, tightly covered, in the refrigerator for up to 2 days before serving.

Yield: 1 1/4 cups

Bertha Nelson, Sherrill O'Neal

KING GASPARILLA XLVII SALAD

Created and graciously shared by James L. Ferman, Sr.

2 large heads of lettuce
3 ribs celery, chopped
¹/₂ cup finely chopped salted
peanuts
4 to 5 ounces dried beef, shredded

4 slices crisp-cooked bacon,
crumbled
1 (8-ounce) jar bleu cheese
salad dressing

All the ingredients should be cold before assembling the salad. Rinse the lettuce and dry well. Shred the lettuce. Combine the lettuce and celery in a large salad bowl and toss to mix. Add the peanuts, dried beef and bacon and toss to mix. Add the salad dressing just before serving and toss to coat.

Variation: For variety, add other leafy vegetables, shredded carrots, chopped cucumbers, tomatoes or onions in any combination.

Yield: 6 servings

Martha Ferman, Charter Member

TELLING TIME

The call to work and the quitting whistle were one and the same and could be heard for a mile. During construction of the hotel, the timekeeper had hung a large circular saw blade outside his office door. To alert the men he banged on it long and hard with an iron pipe.

SALADS

Sweet-Sour Mandarin and Almond Salad

¹/₄ cup sliced almonds

4 teaspoons sugar

¹/₄ head Bibb lettuce

¹/₄ bunch romaine

2 green onions, thinly sliced

Sweet-Sour Salad Dressing

1 (11-ounce) can mandarin
oranges, drained

Place the almonds in a small skillet. Sprinkle with the sugar. Cook over low heat until
the sugar is melted and the almonds are coated, stirring constantly. Spread the almonds on foil.
Let stand until cool, break apart and set aside. Tear the Bibb and romaine lettuces into bite-size
pieces and place in a large plastic bag or salad bowl. Add the green onions and toss until
well mixed. Add the salad dressing and toss until coated. Add the oranges and toss again.
Sprinkle with the sugared almonds just before serving.

Yield: 6 servings

Sweet-Sour Salad Dressing

¹/₄ cup vegetable oil

2 tablespoons sugar

2 tablespoons vinegar

1 tablespoon snipped parsley

¹/₂ teaspoon salt

Pepper and red pepper sauce to taste

Combine the oil, sugar, vinegar, parsley, salt, pepper and pepper sauce in a small
jar and shake vigorously until mixed. Chill in the refrigerator.

Yield: ¹/₂ cup

Patsy Clifford

WATERCRESS SALAD

Watercress for 2 people   Plum tomatoes, chopped
Sliced mushrooms   Garlic and Caper Salad
Toasted almonds   Dressing

Combine the watercress with the desired amounts of mushrooms, toasted almonds and tomatoes in a salad bowl and toss to mix. Add the desired amount of the salad dressing, toss lightly to mix and serve immediately.

Yield: 2 servings

GARLIC AND CAPER SALAD DRESSING

1/3 cup apple cider vinegar   2 cloves of garlic, minced
1 cup extra-virgin olive oil   2 tablespoons grated onion
1 tablespoon salt   1 tablespoon chopped capers
1 tablespoon sugar   1 hard-cooked egg, chopped
1/2 cup chopped fresh parsley   Dash of cayenne

Combine the vinegar, olive oil, salt and sugar in a small bowl and whisk until the salt and sugar dissolve. Add the parsley, garlic, onion, capers, egg and cayenne and mix well. Store the dressing in a covered container in the refrigerator.

Yield: 1 3/4 cups

Patty Ayala

CHUTNEY CHICKEN SALAD

4¹/2 cups chopped cooked chicken
³/4 cup mayonnaise
¹/3 cup chutney
¹/4 teaspoon salt

1¹/2 teaspoons curry powder
1 tablespoon lime juice
1¹/2 cups sliced almonds, toasted
Apple slices

Place the chicken in a large bowl. Mix the mayonnaise, chutney, salt, curry powder and lime juice in a small bowl. Add the mayonnaise mixture to the chicken and mix gently. Chill, covered, until serving time. Add the almonds and toss lightly. Garnish with the apple slices.

Yield: 6 to 8 servings

Martha Ward

TROPICAL CHICKEN SALAD

1 papaya
1 mango
Lemon juice to taste
2 chicken breasts, cooked
1 bunch green onions, chopped

2 ribs celery, chopped
1/2 cup nonfat plain yogurt
¹/2 cup mayonnaise
1 tablespoon curry powder
1 tablespoon ground cumin

Peel the papaya and mango, cut into small bite-size pieces and place in a bowl. Sprinkle with lemon juice to prevent darkening. Cut the chicken into pieces. Add the chicken, green onions and celery to the fruit mixture. Blend the yogurt, mayonnaise, curry powder and cumin in a small bowl. Add to the chicken mixture and mix gently. Chill until serving time.

Yield: 4 to 6 servings

Jane Carswell

QUEEN ELIZABETH CHICKEN SALAD

This was served to Queen Elizabeth in the rotunda of the University of Virginia, Charlottesville.

2 cups chopped cooked
chicken breasts
1/4 cup sliced water chestnuts
1/2 cup chopped celery
1/2 cup slivered almonds, toasted

1 (8-ounce) can pineapple
chunks, drained
8 ounces seedless green grapes,
cut into halves
Curry Dressing

Combine the chicken, water chestnuts, celery and almonds in a bowl. Add the pineapple and grapes and toss lightly to mix. Add the dressing and toss lightly to coat. Chill, covered, for several hours until serving time. Serve the salad on lettuce-lined salad plates. This recipe can be easily doubled or tripled.

Yield: 8 servings

CURRY DRESSING

3/4 cup mayonnaise
2 teaspoons soy sauce

2 teaspoons lemon juice
1 teaspoon curry powder

Blend the mayonnaise, soy sauce, lemon juice and curry powder in a small bowl. May chill before adding to the salad.

Yield: 3/4 cup

Joanne Baldy, Pat Schiff, Marion Wooten

SUMMER CRAB MEAT AND SHRIMP SALAD

1½ cups lump crab meat
1 pound cooked peeled shrimp
½ cup chopped green bell pepper
1 small onion, finely chopped
2 tablespoons minced pimento

¾ cup mayonnaise
3 tablespoons Worcestershire sauce
1 teaspoon salt, or to taste
Lettuce
1 cup chow mein noodles

Combine the crab meat, shrimp, green pepper, onion and pimento in a bowl and toss lightly to mix. Blend the next 3 ingredients in a small bowl. Add to the seafood mixture and toss lightly. Spoon the salad onto lettuce-lined plates. Sprinkle with the chow mein noodles.
Variation: Spoon the salad mixture into a lightly greased casserole, sprinkle with chow mein noodles and bake at 350 degrees for 25 to 30 minutes.

Yield: 4 servings

Vera Swirbul

EASY TUNA SALAD SURPRISE

1 (6-ounce) can tuna
1 (8-ounce) can crushed pineapple
¾ cup chopped celery

¼ to ½ cup chopped nuts
Mayonnaise to taste

Drain the tuna and the pineapple. Place the tuna in a bowl and flake. Add the pineapple, celery and nuts. Add enough mayonnaise to make the salad of the desired consistency. Serve with thin crisp French fries.

Yield: 4 to 6 servings

Mary Pope

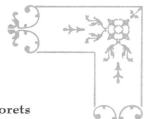

SEAFOOD PASTA SALAD

1 pound rotini	8 ounces small broccoli florets
2¹/₂ tablespoons olive oil	1 (7-ounce) jar pitted Spanish olives,
1 pound medium shrimp	drained, cut into halves
2 (12-ounce) cans lite beer	1 cup slivered almonds
Juice of 1 large lemon	1 (16-ounce) bottle fat-free Italian
1 pound bay scallops	Parmesan salad dressing
10 mushrooms, sliced	Oregano and garlic powder to taste

Cook the rotini according to the package directions adding the olive oil to the boiling water. Drain the rotini, rinse with cold water, drain well and set aside in a large bowl. Bring a generous amount of water to a boil in a large saucepan. Add the shrimp. Cook for about 5 minutes or until the shrimp turn pink; do not overcook. Drain the shrimp well. Pour the beer over the hot shrimp. Let stand for 5 to 10 minutes. Pour off the beer. Peel the shrimp and cut into halves. Place the shrimp in a bowl, sprinkle with about half the lemon juice and chill in the refrigerator. Bring a generous amount of water to a boil in a large saucepan. Add the scallops. Cook for several minutes or until the scallops are opaque. Drain well, place in a bowl and sprinkle with the remaining lemon juice. Chill in the refrigerator. Add the shrimp, scallops, mushrooms, broccoli, olives and almonds to the rotini and toss lightly to mix. Blend the desired amount of salad dressing with oregano and garlic powder. Add the dressing to the seafood mixture and toss lightly. Serve on Bibb lettuce-lined plates with rolls or crackers.

Yield: 8 to 10 servings

Sarah Charles Stevens

SEASIDE RICE SALAD

2 cups cooked chilled rice
1/2 cup cooked crab meat, lobster
or shrimp
1/2 cup slivered Virginia ham
2 hard-cooked eggs, finely chopped
1 tablespoon chopped chives

1/4 cup finely chopped fresh parsley
1 tablespoon olive oil
1 tablespoon wine vinegar
1/2 cup mayonnaise
Salt and pepper to taste

Mix the first 6 ingredients in a salad bowl. Sprinkle with a mixture of the olive oil and vinegar. Add mayonnaise, salt and pepper and mix lightly. Chill, covered, for several hours. Serve with beef, pork or chicken or with Florentine tomatoes or asparagus.

Yield: 6 servings

Pat Martin

BLACK BEAN AND RICE SALAD

1 (15-ounce) can black beans
1 1/2 cups chopped fresh tomatoes
1/2 cup chopped celery
1 cup sliced green onions

2 tablespoons chopped fresh parsley
1 1/2 cups cooked rice
4 ounces feta cheese, crumbled
1/2 cup Italian salad dressing

Rinse and drain the beans. Combine the beans, tomatoes, celery, green onions, parsley, rice and feta cheese in a salad bowl and toss lightly until well mixed. Add the salad dressing and toss to mix. Chill, covered, for at least 2 hours before serving.

Yield: 5 servings

Gwen Young

SALADS

CURRIED RICE SALAD

1 (7-ounce) package chicken-flavored
    Rice-A-Roni
2 (6-ounce) jars marinated
    artichoke hearts
$^{1}/_{3}$ cup mayonnaise

$^{3}/_{4}$ teaspoon curry powder
$^{1}/_{2}$ cup chopped green or red
    bell peppers
3 green onions, chopped
24 pimento-stuffed olives, sliced

Cook the Rice-A-Roni using package directions and let stand until cool. Drain the artichokes, reserving the liquid from one jar. Blend the reserved liquid with the mayonnaise and curry powder in a bowl. Mix with the Rice-A-Roni in a salad bowl. Add the remaining ingredients and mix lightly. Chill, covered, until serving time.

Yield: 6 servings

Anne Robbins Butler, Friend of the Chiselers

NO-FAT BOILED SALAD DRESSING

$^{2}/_{3}$ cup sugar
1 tablespoon dry mustard
3 tablespoons cornstarch
1 teaspoon salt

$1^{1}/_{2}$ cups cold water
3 eggs, beaten
1 cup cider vinegar

Mix the first 4 ingredients in a double boiler. Blend in the cold water. Cook over boiling water until thickened, stirring constantly. Beat the eggs and vinegar in a medium bowl. Stir a small amount of the hot mixture into the eggs; stir the eggs into the hot mixture. Reduce heat to low. Cook until thickened, stirring frequently. Cool. Store in an airtight glass jar.

Yield: 3 cups

Marjorie Christopher

POPPY SEED DRESSING

1/3 cup sugar
1 teaspoon dry mustard
1 teaspoon salt
5 1/2 tablespoons vinegar

1 cup vegetable oil
2 1/2 teaspoons poppy seeds
1 1/2 teaspoons grated onion

Combine the sugar, dry mustard, salt and vinegar in a blender container and process until well mixed. Add the oil in a fine stream, processing constantly. Mix in the poppy seeds and onion. Store the dressing in a tightly closed container in the refrigerator. Use the dressing over a fresh fruit salad served on a bed of crisp lettuce.

Yield: 1 1/2 cups

Sarah Wahl

CRAFTSMANSHIP

After the great hotel had been built, the architect's chief assistant marveled at the skill of his crewmen: "We had no level instrument [but] it was found that in twelve hundred feet, the length of the building, there was less than a course of brick out of level, a remarkable showing in any building."

SALADS

LOW-FAT VINAIGRETTE

In the search for a low-fat salad dressing, my husband, Simeon, came up with this.

¼ cup red wine vinegar
¼ cup balsamic vinegar
¼ cup dry red wine
1 tablespoon honey
½ cup extra-virgin olive oil
2 to 3 cloves of garlic, pressed
½ teaspoon crushed dried basil

1 teaspoon crushed dried oregano
1 teaspoon dry mustard
½ teaspoon black pepper
¼ teaspoon ground bay leaf
¼ teaspoon ground celery seeds
1½ cans jellied beef consommé

Combine the vinegars, wine, honey and olive oil in a 1-quart jar. Add the garlic, basil, oregano, dry mustard, pepper, bay leaf and celery seeds. Cover the jar and shake vigorously. Add the consommé and shake until well mixed. Refrigerate for 4 to 5 hours. Shake well and adjust to taste by adding a small amount of additional vinegar or oil. Store, tightly covered, in the refrigerator. Shake well before each use.

Yield: 1 quart

Marion Wooten

Soups
&
Side Dishes

*Guests take their ease amidst
princely antiques in the
hotel's Grand Salon.*

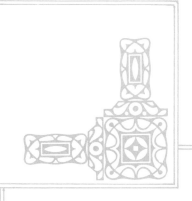

The
Grand Salon

They said that the hotel's
Grand Salon was beyond compare.
One curved wall was set with tall windows festooned in silk, there were two elaborate fireplaces
and an oval dome, proudly ringed with 64 bare light bulbs, soared above all. But they were talking
about the furniture. The Salon was quite full of ornate tables and chests, chairs and settees,
each one carved, joined and polished by the hand of a master. But the hotel guests were not
the first to enjoy the jewel-like quality of the furnishings, for all had been purchased from the
finest dealers of antiquities in Europe and the Orient. Masterful oil paintings adorned the walls
of the Salon, chests were surmounted with prized porcelains and amidst the clutter of furniture
stood statuary cast in bronze. The walls of this marvelous room glittered with carved Florentine and
Venetian mirrors—one could have counted 110 of them throughout the hotel—and great oriental
jardinieres were set about. The Plants had sent home 80 carloads of precious objects from their
two-year buying trip and when the rooms began to overflow with antiques,
Plant was obliged to auction off some of the last shipment. But it is said that he kept back a table
containing 1400 pieces of inlaid wood and could not part with a matched pair of green Tibetan
vases banded with crushed emeralds. With the demise of the hotel, some of the princely furnishings
were removed by Henry Plant's heirs, other pieces discreetly disappeared and not a
few tables and chairs were lost forever,
carelessly burned as firewood.

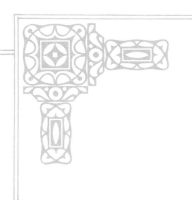

ASPARAGUS AND CRAB MEAT BISQUE

1 (10-ounce) can cream of
mushroom soup
1 (10-ounce) can cream of
asparagus soup

1 cup water
1 1/2 cups half-and-half
1 (6-ounce) can crab meat,
drained

Combine the canned soups, water and half-and-half in a large saucepan and
stir until well mixed. Add the crab meat and mix well. Cook over medium-low heat
until heated to serving temperature, stirring frequently.

Yield: 4 servings

Pat Colvard

LEAF AND BLOSSOM DESIGN

*In the late 1880s, Neo-Gothic elements found expression in
furniture and architectural design, such as the combining of leaf and blossom
motifs into rectangular shapes, like this pattern repeated
on the hotel woodwork.*

Frijoles Negros

All my life we had black beans and rice at least monthly. My father's family was from Spain, and my mother, born to a Florida pioneer family, learned to cook most of the things he liked.

2 pounds dry black beans
1 pound meaty ham hocks
5 ounces salt pork
9 bay leaves
1 tablespoon crushed oregano
4 large Spanish onions, chopped

4 to 6 cloves of garlic, chopped
9 green bell peppers, chopped
2 cups olive oil
3 tablespoons salt
1/2 cup vinegar

Sort the beans and rinse thoroughly. Place the beans in a 3- to 4-quart soup pot. Add enough water to cover the beans with about 2 inches of water. Soak the beans overnight. Add additional water to cover the beans by 1 inch. Cut the ham hocks and salt pork into small pieces and add to the beans. Add the bay leaves and oregano. Bring to a boil over medium heat, skim and reduce the heat to low. Simmer, covered, for about 1 hour or until the beans are tender. Sauté the onions, garlic and green peppers in the olive oil in a large skillet until tender. Add to the beans. Simmer, covered, until the mixture is of the desired consistency, stirring occasionally. Add the salt if needed and stir in the vinegar just before serving. Discard the bay leaves. Serve buffet-style with yellow rice. Supply carafes of olive oil and vinegar for individual service.

Yield: variable

Helen Davis

A Yankee's Spanish Bean Soup

*After first tasting Ybor City's Spanish Bean Soup, I experimented
until I found the same flavor. The Vigo in the recipe is a mixture of saffron and
other spices and gives the soup a yellow color. I make this after the
ham has been enjoyed and only the hock remains.*

1 pound dry garbanzos
1 meaty ham hock
1 large onion, chopped
1 green bell pepper, chopped
2 to 3 cloves of garlic, chopped

3 or 4 bay leaves
3 or 4 white potatoes,
   finely chopped
2 packets Vigo flavoring
   and coloring

Sort the garbanzos and rinse thoroughly. Place the garbanzos in a large saucepan or soup
pot. Cover generously with water. Soak the garbanzos overnight. Drain the garbanzos. Add the
ham hock, onion, green pepper, garlic and bay leaves to the pot. Add enough water to cover
generously. Simmer, covered, until the garbanzos are tender. Add the potatoes and Vigo
and simmer until the potatoes are tender. Discard the bay leaves.
Variations: If the ham is in short supply, add some chopped chorizos for added flavor.
Using a pressure cooker will reduce the cooking time but add the potatoes and
Vigo last and cook just long enough to cook the potatoes.

Yield: 6 to 8 servings

Lynn Carlton

HEARTY CABBAGE AND BEAN SOUP

We had enjoyed a similar soup at a restaurant in North Georgia. When I asked the waitress how it was made, she named the key ingredients and this is the result. My family loves it on a chilly day.

1 1/2 pounds lean ground beef
2 tablespoons olive oil
2 cups chopped onions
2 cloves of garlic, minced
1 tablespoon olive oil
2 (14-ounce) cans beef broth
2 teaspoons lemon juice

1 (28-ounce) can crushed
  tomatoes
1 to 2 tablespoons brown sugar
1/4 teaspoon pepper
4 cups shredded cabbage
2 (15-ounce) cans kidney beans

Cook the ground beef in 2 tablespoons olive oil in a large soup pot or Dutch oven until brown and crumbly, stirring frequently. Drain the ground beef and set aside. Sauté the onions and garlic in 1 tablespoon olive oil in the soup pot until tender; drain. Return the ground beef to the pot. Add the broth, lemon juice, tomatoes, brown sugar and pepper and mix well. Bring to a boil and reduce the heat. Simmer, covered, for 45 minutes. Add the cabbage. Drain and rinse the beans. Add the beans to the pot. Return to a boil and reduce the heat. Simmer, covered, for 25 to 30 minutes.

Yield: 10 servings

Jane Hewit

Santa Fe Soup

*Much like stew, this is a great company dish served with
salad and bread . . . and is fairly low-fat, too.*

2 pounds ground turkey or
ground beef
1 onion, chopped
2 (.5-ounce) envelopes ranch-style
salad dressing mix
2 (1.25-ounce) envelopes taco
seasoning mix
1 (16-ounce) can black beans

1 (16-ounce) can kidney beans
1 (16-ounce) can pinto beans
1 (16-ounce) can tomatoes with
green chiles
1 (16-ounce) can diced tomatoes
2 (16-ounce) cans white corn
2 cups water

Cook the ground turkey and onion in a large soup pot until brown and crumbly, stirring
frequently. Add the salad dressing mix and taco seasoning mix and mix well. Add the undrained
black, kidney and pinto beans and mix well. Add the undrained tomatoes with green chiles,
tomatoes and corn. Stir in the water. Simmer, covered, for 2 hours, stirring occasionally and
adding a small amount of water if necessary to make the soup of the desired consistency. Ladle
into soup bowls. Garnish individual servings to taste with dollops of sour cream, shredded
Cheddar cheese and sliced green onions. Serve with tortilla chips.

Yield: 12 to 20 servings

Holli Morris

Broccoli Cheese Soup

¾ cup chopped onion	1 teaspoon salt
2 tablespoons butter or margarine	1 (10-ounce) package frozen chopped
5 cups water	broccoli
6 chicken bouillon cubes	6 cups warm milk
8 ounces wide noodles	1 pound Velveeta cheese, cubed

Sauté the onion in butter in a large soup pot until tender. Add the water and bouillon cubes. Bring to a boil and boil for 5 minutes or until the bouillon cubes are dissolved, stirring frequently. Add the noodles and salt. Cook until the noodles are tender. Add the broccoli. Cook for several minutes longer or until the broccoli is tender. Stir the warm milk into the broccoli mixture gradually. Add the cheese. Cook until the cheese is melted, stirring frequently. Refrigerate the soup for 8 to 12 hours to develop the flavor. Reheat over medium-low heat, stirring frequently.

Yield: 8 to 10 servings

Jane Hewit

Tips Not Included

In its 1896 brochure, the hotel unabashedly described itself as "a thing of beauty within and without, a monument typifying what lavish expenditure, exquisite taste and ideal surroundings can accomplish when properly directed." The advertisement, however, shied from mentioning the price of enjoying a night in these extravagant surroundings. But records reveal that when the hotel opened in 1891, a bedroom furnished with European antiques was billed at $5 per night and suite with private bath, $18.

CUCUMBER GOBLETS

This refreshing soup was served at the President's house—Michigan State.

4 medium cucumbers	2 tablespoons cold water
1 small onion, chopped	2 cups half-and-half or skim milk
2 cups chicken broth	2 tablespoons chopped fresh dill
2 tablespoons cornstarch	

Peel the cucumbers and cut into halves lengthwise. Scoop out and discard the seeds and chop the cucumbers coarsely. Combine the cucumbers, onion and broth in a saucepan. Bring to a boil and reduce the heat. Simmer, covered, for 5 minutes or until tender. Pour into a blender container and process until smooth. Return the cucumber mixture to the saucepan. Dissolve the cornstarch in the cold water. Stir into the cucumber mixture. Bring to a boil, stirring constantly. Reduce the heat and simmer for 3 to 5 minutes, stirring frequently. Let stand until cool. Blend in the half-and-half. Stir in the dill. Chill in the refrigerator until serving time. Serve in mugs or crystal goblets.

Yield: 6 to 8 servings

Anita Gillen

MUSHROOM BARLEY SOUP

A favorite menu item at Yesterdays restaurant in Cashiers, North Carolina.
The restaurant no longer exists, but it is missed.

1 large onion, chopped
12 ounces mushrooms, sliced
½ cup butter
2 tablespoons flour
8 cups chicken broth

¾ cup quick-cooking medium
   barley
2 cups milk
1 cup half-and-half
White pepper and salt to taste

Sauté the onion and mushrooms in butter in a large saucepan over medium heat until the onion is tender. Sprinkle with the flour. Cook for about 3 minutes, stirring constantly. Stir in the broth and barley. Bring to a boil, stirring constantly and reduce the heat. Simmer, covered, for 45 minutes. Stir in the milk and half-and-half gradually. Cook at the barely simmering stage for 30 minutes. Add pepper and salt. Serve in heated soup bowls.

Yield: 8 servings

Jane Watson

Fresh Mushroom Bisque

1/4 cup minced celery

1/4 cup minced onion

2 tablespoons corn oil

2 1/2 tablespoons flour

1 cup boiling chicken broth

1 1/2 cups warm low-fat or
whole milk

1/2 teaspoon salt

1/8 teaspoon ground nutmeg

1/4 teaspoon white pepper

1/2 teaspoon tarragon

4 teaspoons margarine

2 cups thinly sliced mushrooms

2 tablespoons sherry (optional)

1/2 cup minced fresh parsley

2 tablespoons toasted almond
flakes

Sauté the celery and onion in corn oil in a large saucepan until tender. Add the flour. Cook for about 3 minutes, stirring constantly; do not brown. Add the boiling broth all at once and whisk briskly until well mixed. Cook until thickened, whisking constantly. Stir in the warm milk gradually. Add the salt, nutmeg, pepper and tarragon and mix well. Heat to serving temperature over low heat, stirring occasionally. Melt the margarine in a heavy skillet. Add the mushrooms and sauté until tender. Add the mushrooms to the soup. Add the sherry. Ladle into soup bowls and sprinkle with the parsley and almond flakes.

Yield: 8 servings

Sherrill O'Neal

PASTA FAGIOLI

4 cloves of garlic, chopped
1/4 cup olive oil
2 (14-ounce) cans tomatoes
3 cups chicken broth
2 bay leaves
2 teaspoons each oregano and thyme

1 teaspoon salt
Pepper to taste
3 (14-ounce) cans Great Northern
    beans, drained, rinsed
~~8 ounces elbow macaroni, cooked~~
cooked sausage (1 lb)

Sauté the garlic in olive oil in a large soup pot. Process the tomatoes in a blender and add to the soup pot with the broth and seasonings. Simmer for 15 minutes. Add the beans and macaroni. Simmer for 30 minutes. Discard the bay leaves.

Yield: 6 to 8 servings

Judy Rodriguez

CREAM OF PEANUT SOUP

1 medium onion, chopped
2 ribs celery, chopped
1/4 cup butter
3 tablespoons flour

2 quarts chicken broth
2 cups creamy peanut butter
1 3/4 cups light cream

Sauté the onion and celery in the butter in a saucepan. Stir in the flour. Add the broth and bring to a boil, stirring constantly. Purée the mixture in a blender. Blend with the peanut butter and cream in the saucepan. Heat to serving temperature over low heat; do not boil. Ladle into soup bowls and garnish with a sprinkle of chopped peanuts.

Yield: 8 to 10 servings

Beverly Rogers

SICILIAN SEAFOOD CHOWDER

1/2 cup chopped onion

1/2 cup chopped celery

1/2 cup chopped green bell pepper

3 tablespoons olive oil

3 large cloves of garlic, minced

1/2 teaspoon crushed dried basil

1/2 teaspoon crushed dried thyme

1/4 teaspoon crushed dried oregano

1/4 teaspoon crushed dried red pepper flakes

1/2 teaspoon black pepper

2 1/2 cups bottled clam juice

1 (15-ounce) can tomato sauce

2 ounces orzo

8 ounces uncooked medium shrimp, peeled, deveined

8 ounces sea scallops

1 (6-ounce) can chopped clams, drained

1 tablespoon chopped fresh parsley

Sauté the onion, celery and green pepper in olive oil in a large saucepan over medium-high heat for about 7 minutes. Add the garlic, basil, thyme, oregano, red pepper flakes and black pepper. Cook for 2 minutes, stirring frequently. Stir in the clam juice and tomato sauce. Bring to a boil and reduce the heat. Simmer for about 30 minutes or until slightly thickened, stirring occasionally. (Soup may be prepared to this point and refrigerated until the next day if desired. Bring the mixture to a simmer before proceeding.) Cook the orzo al dente using the package directions; drain. Rinse with cold water, drain well and set aside. Add the shrimp and scallops to the chowder. Cook just for 4 minutes or until the shrimp turn pink and the scallops are opaque. Add the orzo, clams and parsley and mix well. Heat to serving temperature and ladle into soup bowls.

Yield: 6 servings

Emalou Grable

SPINACH SOUP

2 (10-ounce) packages frozen chopped spinach
4 chicken bouillon cubes
4 cups light cream

¼ cup dry vermouth
½ teaspoon ground mace
1 teaspoon grated lemon rind
2 hard-cooked eggs, chopped

Cook the spinach using the package directions just until tender. Drain and squeeze dry. Purée in a blender or food processor and set aside. Combine the bouillon cubes and cream in a large saucepan and heat over medium-high heat until the cream is scalded and the bouillon cubes have dissolved, stirring constantly. Remove from the heat. Add the spinach purée, vermouth, mace and lemon rind and mix well. Chill until serving time. Sprinkle servings with the chopped egg.

Yield: 6 servings

Marion Wooten

THE PLEASURE OF YOUR COMPANY

The roar of a cannon competed with the hotel orchestra's lively music. Guests were elegantly attired befitting the grandeur of the occasion, the gentlemen sporting handlebar mustaches and top hats and their ladies bustled in satin and lace. "They began to arrive at the west portico, a great many in carriages, but a large number walked. . . ." read a contemporary account of the formal-dress opening of the hotel in February of 1891. "The stars shone forth with radiance, unobserved by even a fleecy cloud. . . . From the city bridge the sight was beautiful beyond description . . . a panoramic view of fairyland, every front room of the caravansary brightly illuminated with incandescent electric lights!" Fifteen thousand persons had received engraved invitations to this Opening Ball, and 300 employees were on hand to welcome the guests.

SOUPS & SIDE DISHES

KAHLÚA SPICED PEACHES

2 (29-ounce) cans cling peach halves
½ cup Kahlúa
½ cup packed brown sugar
¼ cup tarragon white wine vinegar

2 cinnamon sticks
3 thin (4-inch) strips orange rind
3 thin (4-inch) strips lemon rind

Drain the peaches, reserving the liquid. Pour 1½ cups of the reserved liquid into a saucepan. Pour the peach halves into a bowl. Add the remaining ingredients to the saucepan. Simmer for 5 to 6 minutes. Pour over the peach halves. Let stand until cool. Store, covered, in the refrigerator for up to several weeks.

Yield: 12 to 14 servings

Sarah Wahl

SCALLOPED PINEAPPLE

2 cups sugar
¾ cup melted margarine
3 eggs or the equivalent
    egg substitute

2 tablespoons milk
1 (20-ounce) can crushed
    pineapple
4 cups soft bread crumbs (7 slices)

Blend the sugar and margarine in a large bowl. Add the eggs and milk and mix well. Fold in the undrained pineapple and bread crumbs. Pour into a greased 2½-quart casserole. Bake at 350 degrees for 1 hour or until the top is golden brown and the casserole is set. Let stand for 5 to 10 minutes before serving. This is a great side dish with turkey or ham.

Yield: 8 to 10 servings

Vicki Hussey

Corn Bread Dressing

1 pan corn bread, crumbled	½ cup melted butter
8 slices dry white bread, torn	1 to 2 cups chicken broth
1 cup chopped onion	1 to 2 cups water
1 cup chopped celery	Salt to taste
5 hard-cooked eggs, chopped	

Combine the corn bread and white bread in a large bowl. Add the onion, celery, eggs and butter and mix well. Add enough of the broth and water to make the mixture of the desired consistency; the mixture should be very moist. Add salt as desired. Pour into a greased 9x11-inch baking pan. Bake, covered, at 375 degrees for 30 minutes. Bake, uncovered, for 15 minutes longer.

Yield: 10 to 12 servings

Ginger Tarr Shea

Number, Please?

Alexander Graham Bell's sizable invention did not quite meet Henry Bradley Plant's standard of aesthetics. Therefore, the hotelier requested that the Bell Telephone Company design a smaller instrument exclusively for use in his resort on Tampa Bay. And so a diminutive vulcanized rubber device ornamented the wall of each hotel room, guests having to but press a button to speak to any of the staff standing ready to serve. And what pleasures might be rung for: fresh crab and Champagne to quell hunger, a hot water bottle wrapped in flannel to warm linen sheets. And should madame yearn for music, attendants would most gladly rush a piano to her room.

Garlic Cheese Grits

This recipe can be prepared ahead of time, but do not pop it in the oven until you are sure you can serve it the minute it comes out. It should have the consistency of spoon bread.

2 cups grits	1/2 cup butter
6 cups water	4 eggs, beaten
1/2 cup milk	Salt, pepper, Parmesan cheese and
2 (6-ounce) rolls garlic cheese	paprika to taste

Cook the grits in boiling water using the package directions. Remove from the heat. Add the milk, garlic cheese and butter and stir until the cheese and butter are melted. Add the eggs, salt and pepper and mix well. Pour into a buttered 9x13-inch baking dish. Sprinkle generously with Parmesan cheese and paprika. Bake at 300 degrees for 30 minutes.

Yield: 10 to 12 servings

Holli Morris

Oven Hominy

2 (16-ounce) cans white hominy	1 cup sour cream
1 cup shredded Monterey Jack cheese	1 cup chopped green chiles, drained

Drain the hominy, rinse and drain well. Combine the hominy with the cheese, sour cream and green chiles and mix well. Pour into a greased baking dish. Bake at 350 degrees for 25 minutes.

Yield: 6 servings

Dot Trigg

LINGUINI WITH OLIVE OIL AND GARLIC

1 pound linguini	³/4 cup Italian olive oil
¹/4 cup water	¹/2 cup corn oil
1 bulb garlic, chopped	2 tablespoons chopped parsley
1 tablespoon salt	Parmesan cheese to taste

Cook the linguini al dente using the package directions. Bring ¹/4 cup water to a simmer in a 4¹/2-quart pan. Add the hot drained linguini to the pot, cover and set aside. Sauté the garlic with salt in a mixture of olive oil and corn oil in a large skillet over medium-high heat until the garlic is golden brown. Pour the garlic mixture over the linguini, add the parsley and toss until well mixed. Serve immediately with generous amounts of Parmesan cheese.

Yield: 8 servings

Judy Rodriguez

A FLICK OF THE SWITCH

An early guest at the hotel wrote home, "In the bedrooms there are various things that are not to be found elsewhere. Here is my own, for instance; step in and see what we can find. . . . Here is a circular mirror, about a foot and a half inches in diameter, set in the ceiling with a cluster of three electric lights immediately under it. When these are turned on there is not merely a glitter of light in one part of the room and darkness all around, but the whole room is made brilliant, from floor to ceiling!!"
from the New York Times
January 24, 1892

"And They Called it Macaroni"

I've been making this recipe since I married in 1939.
It can be served as a meatless entrée or side dish.

¹/₂ cup uncooked macaroni	¹/₄ cup butter
12 ounces sharp Cheddar cheese, shredded	3 eggs, lightly beaten
¹/₄ cup chopped green bell pepper	1 cup milk
¹/₄ cup grated onion	1 (2-ounce) jar chopped pimento, drained
1 (2-ounce) can mushroom pieces, drained	Salt and pepper to taste
	2 tablespoons buttered bread crumbs

Cook the macaroni using the package directions. Drain well and add the cheese to the hot macaroni. Mix until the cheese melts and set the macaroni aside. Sauté the green pepper, onion and mushrooms in butter in a skillet until tender. Drain the sautéed vegetables and add to the macaroni. Beat the eggs with the milk and add to the macaroni and mix well. Stir in the pimento, salt and pepper. Pour the mixture into a buttered casserole. Sprinkle the buttered crumbs over the top. Place the casserole in a larger pan half filled with hot water. Bake at 350 degrees for 1 hour or until a knife inserted in the center comes out clean.

Yield: 6 servings

Margery Starns

WILD RICE PARTY DISH

¹/₂ cup butter
1 cup wild rice or long grain and
wild rice mix without seasonings
2 tablespoons minced onion
8 ounces mushrooms, sliced

¹/₂ cup slivered almonds
1 teaspoon salt
3 cups chicken broth
2 tablespoons sherry

Melt the butter in a large skillet. Add the rice, onion, mushrooms and almonds.
Sauté until the mixture is light brown and well coated with the butter.
Season with the salt. Spoon the mixture into a 1½-quart casserole. Add the broth
and sherry and mix well. Cover the casserole tightly. Bake at 325 degrees for
1 hour or until the rice is tender. The casserole may be frozen before baking
but be sure to return to room temperature before baking.

Yield: 6 servings

Francine Dobkin

STEAK RICE

1 1/2 cups long grain rice
1/2 cup margarine
1 (10-ounce) can French onion soup
1/2 cup beef broth
1/2 cup water
1 cup dry vermouth

1 (8-ounce) jar sliced mushrooms, drained
1 (8-ounce) can sliced water chestnuts, drained
Salt and lemon pepper to taste

Sauté the rice in margarine in a large skillet until brown. Add the remaining ingredients and mix well. Pour into a 2-quart casserole. Bake, covered, at 325 degrees for 1 1/4 hours. Increase the oven temperature to 350 degrees. Bake, uncovered, for 15 minutes longer.

Yield: 8 servings

Mary Anne Ingram

WILD RICE WITH OLIVES

1 cup wild rice
1 cup chopped black olives
1 (20-ounce) can stewed tomatoes
1 (2-ounce) can sliced mushrooms
1/2 cup olive oil

1 1/2 teaspoons salt
1/2 teaspoon pepper
1 1/2 cups boiling water
1 cup shredded sharp Cheddar cheese

Mix the wild rice, olives, tomatoes, mushrooms, olive oil, salt and pepper in a 9x13-inch baking pan. Drizzle the boiling water over the mixture. Sprinkle with the cheese. Bake at 350 degrees for 1 1/2 hours, adding small amounts of hot water as necessary.

Yield: 8 servings

Beth Arthur

FLORIDA WILD RICE

1 1/2 cups chopped onion
3/4 cup mixed chopped red and green
    bell peppers
3/4 cup butter
6 cups cooked wild rice
3 cups sliced mushrooms
1/4 cup butter
3 tablespoons olive oil
1 tablespoon Worcestershire sauce

1/2 teaspoon seasoned salt
1 cup dried cherries
1 cup pecans, toasted, chopped
1/4 cup mixed chopped fresh herbs such
    as basil, chives, dill and coriander
1 tablespoon slivered orange rind,
    chopped
Salt and pepper to taste

Sauté the onion and bell peppers in 3/4 cup butter in a skillet until tender. Combine with the wild rice in a large bowl. Keep warm. Sauté the mushrooms in a mixture of 1/4 cup butter and the olive oil in the skillet until tender. Add the Worcestershire sauce and seasoned salt, mix well and add to the rice mixture. Add the dried cherries, pecans, herbs, orange rind, salt and pepper and mix well. Serve immediately.

Yield: 10 servings

Adajean Samson

MAIN DISHES

Maisie arrives at the Tampa Bay Hotel.

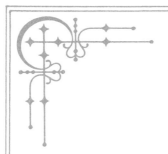
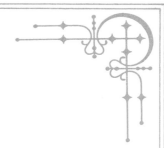

MAISIE'S PEARLS

Maisie knew to the penny how much her new husband loved her.
Hadn't Morton Plant paid her first husband $8 million
to divorce her, so he might have her for his very own, to love,
protect and shower gifts upon? And hadn't he bought her a mansion
on fashionable Fifth Avenue in which he and Maisie would enjoy
with proper splendor a life befitting their role in New York society?
Morton may have learned generosity from his father, Henry B. Plant,
but he was no spendthrift. And so when his wife coveted the stunning
double rope of pearls showcased in Cartier's window, Morton balked
at its equally stunning price tag.
Rare and gorgeous though the pearls were, Morton said no.
And, pray, what recourse exists for a gentlewoman of high rank whose
heart's desire has been thwarted by the very man who lavished so much of life's
luxuries upon her? Overpriced though the necklace may be, there was naught
to do but that Maisie take matters into her own hands.
Determined to have her pearls, Maisie ordered her driver to take her
once again to Cartier's. A portrait painted not long afterwards shows a poised
and bejeweled Maisie, with that very necklace of exceedingly large and glowing pearls
resting proudly upon her silken decolletage. And it is no coincidence that Cartier
had just become the new owner of Maisie Plant's wedding-present mansion,
an address the famous jewelers have retained to this day.

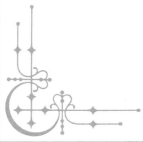
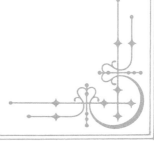

Beef au Poivre

This is Chef Helen Corbitt's famous recipe from the Dallas Neiman Marcus Zodiac Room. Served rare to medium-rare, it is wonderful.

1 beef ribeye roast or other boneless cut	Salt
Olive oil	¾ cup peppercorns, ground
	1 cup burgundy

Rub the roast with olive oil and salt. Rub the roast with the peppercorns. Place the prepared roast in a roasting pan. Roast at 350 degrees for 1 hour (total roasting time should be calculated at 20 minutes per pound). Pour the burgundy over the roast. Roast for the remaining calculated cooking time, basting frequently with the pan juices. Let stand for several minutes before slicing.

Yield: 6 servings

Pat Martin

Easy Old-Fashioned Pot Roast

1 (3- to 4-pound) boneless chuck roast	1 (10-ounce) can mushroom soup
Salt and pepper to taste	1 package peeled baby carrots
1 envelope beefy onion soup mix	8 to 10 red creamer potatoes

Place the roast in a roaster. Sprinkle with salt, pepper and soup mix. Spread the mushroom soup over the top. Add ½ soup can water to the roaster. Roast, covered, at 325 degrees for 3 hours. Add the carrots and potatoes and a small amount of additional water if needed. Roast, covered, for 1 hour longer.

Yield: 8 servings

Ruthanne McLean

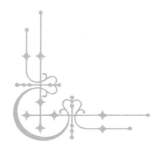

MAIN DISHES

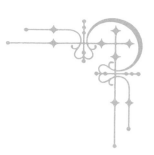

Beef Wellington

1 (4- to 4½-pound) filet of beef, trimmed
Salt and pepper to taste
3¾ cups flour
1½ teaspoons salt
1 cup plus 2 tablespoons butter
¾ cup ice water
1 pound mushrooms, minced
¼ cup minced green onions

¼ cup butter
½ teaspoon marjoram
2 teaspoons flour
Pepper to taste
¼ cup white wine
2 tablespoons minced parsley
½ cup minced ham
1 egg
Sesame seeds to taste

Sprinkle the beef with salt and pepper in a roaster. Roast at 425 degrees for 30 minutes. Let stand until cool. Trim and discard any fat, skin and fascia. Roll tightly in foil, pressing the ends toward the center to shape to the same thickness end to end. Seal tightly. Refrigerate for 8 to 12 hours. Mix 3¾ cups flour and 1 teaspoon of the salt in a bowl. Cut in 1 cup plus 2 tablespoons butter until the mixture is crumbly. Add the ice water and mix until the mixture forms a ball. Chill, tightly covered, for 30 minutes or longer. Sauté the mushrooms and green onions in ¼ cup butter in a large skillet until tender. Add ½ teaspoon salt, marjoram, 2 teaspoons flour and pepper. Stir in the white wine. Bring to a boil, stirring constantly. Stir in the parsley and ham. Chill in the refrigerator. Roll on waxed paper into a rectangle about 12 inches wide and 3 inches longer than the beef. Press the mushroom mixture into the pastry, leaving an inch of pastry uncovered on all edges. Unwrap the beef and place in the center. Trim the ends of the pastry so that a single layer of pastry will cover the ends of the beef. Moisten the pastry edges with water and wrap around the beef, pressing to seal. Place seam side down in a shallow baking pan. Cut decorations from the remaining pastry to press on top. Cover and chill for several hours before baking if desired. Beat the egg with a small amount of water. Brush over the pastry; sprinkle with sesame seeds. Bake at 400 degrees for 25 minutes or until brown. Let stand for 15 minutes.

Yield: 8 servings

Phyllis Kimbel

Main Dishes

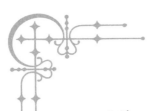

Saucy Beef Filets

1 (6- to 8-pound) beef tenderloin
1 tablespoon salt
1 teaspoon pepper
2 cloves of garlic, crushed
1/2 cup butter
6 to 8 tablespoons flour
6 tablespoons brandy

4 teaspoons tomato paste
2 cloves of garlic, crushed
1 cup beef bouillon
2 cups chicken broth
1 1/2 cups dry red wine
1/4 cup currant jelly
1/2 teaspoon Worcestershire sauce

Cut the tenderloin into 1-inch-thick steaks. Rub the steaks on all sides with salt, pepper and 2 cloves of garlic. Heat 2 tablespoons butter at a time in a skillet. Sear the steaks on all sides in the butter and place in a baking dish. Blend the flour with the pan drippings to make a roux. Add the brandy. Cook until brown, stirring constantly. Add the tomato paste and 2 cloves of garlic and mix well. Remove from the heat and stir in the bouillon, broth, wine, jelly and Worcestershire sauce. Cook until thickened, stirring constantly. Pour the sauce over the steaks. Refrigerate, covered, for 8 to 12 hours or freeze if desired. Bring the steaks to room temperature. Bake at 400 degrees for 15 to 20 minutes for medium.

Yield: 12 servings

Pat Martin

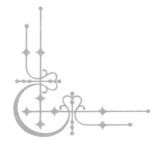

Glazed London Broil

A favorite recipe of KC, the chef at our home in Korea—always delicious and tender!

2 flank steaks	1 teaspoon salt
2 teaspoons unseasoned meat tenderizer	1 teaspoon MSG
	1 teaspoon oregano
1 tablespoon sugar	1/2 teaspoon basil
2 tablespoons dry sherry	1 bay leaf
2 tablespoons soy sauce	12 peppercorns
1 tablespoon honey	

Pierce the steaks at 1-inch intervals with a sharp fork. Place the steaks in a shallow dish. Combine the meat tenderizer, sugar, sherry, soy sauce, honey, salt, MSG, oregano, basil, bay leaf and peppercorns in a small bowl and mix well. Pour over the steaks. Let stand at room temperature for 1 hour, turning frequently. Drain the steaks and place on a rack in a broiler pan. Broil 3 inches from the heat source for 3 minutes on each side. Slice very thinly across the grain.

Yield: 6 to 8 servings

Beverly Rogers

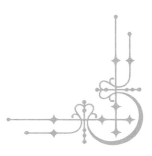

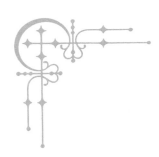

BEEF BOURGUIGNONNE

5 pounds beef chuck	2 tablespoons parsley
Flour to coat	1 bay leaf
1/4 cup butter	1 teaspoon thyme
1/4 cup olive oil	4 cups burgundy
Salt and pepper to taste	1 tablespoon butter, softened
1/4 cup Cognac, warmed	1 tablespoon flour
8 ounces bacon, chopped	36 mushroom caps
3 cloves of garlic, crushed	2 tablespoons butter
2 carrots, chopped	2 tablespoons olive oil
3 cups chopped onions	Juice of 1/2 lemon

Cut the beef into large cubes and roll in flour to coat. Heat 1/4 cup butter and 1/4 cup olive oil in a large skillet over high heat. Add the beef and brown on all sides. Remove from the heat. Sprinkle with salt and pepper and drizzle the Cognac over the top; ignite. Allow the flames to die and place the beef in a large casserole. Sauté the bacon, garlic, carrots, onions and parsley in the skillet until the bacon is crisp and the vegetables are light brown. Add the mixture to the casserole. Add the bay leaf, thyme, burgundy and enough water to cover. Bake, covered, at 350 degrees for 2 hours. Prepare a beurre manié by blending 1 tablespoon softened butter with 1 tablespoon flour. Add to the casserole a very small amount at a time, mixing well after each addition. Bake the casserole, covered, for 2 hours longer. Sauté the mushroom caps in 2 tablespoons butter and 2 tablespoons olive oil until light brown. Sprinkle with lemon juice and sauté for several minutes longer. Spoon the mushrooms over the top of the casserole and serve immediately.

Yield: 10 to 12 servings

Beverly Rogers

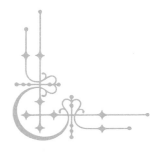

MAIN DISHES

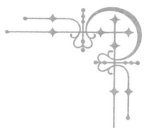

COMPANY BEEF STROGANOFF

1 pound beef tenderloin	2 tablespoons catsup
8 ounces fresh mushrooms, sliced	1 clove of garlic, crushed
1/2 cup minced onion	1 teaspoon salt
2 tablespoons butter	3 tablespoons flour
1 (10-ounce) can beef consommé	1 cup sour cream

Cut the tenderloin into thin strips. Sauté the mushrooms and onion in the butter in a large skillet until tender. Remove the sautéed vegetables from the skillet and add the tenderloin. Cook until brown on all sides, stirring frequently. Reserve 1/3 cup of the consommé. Add the remaining consommé, catsup, garlic and salt to the skillet. Simmer, covered, for 15 minutes. Blend the reserved consommé with the flour and stir into the skillet. Cook until thickened, stirring constantly. Stir in the sautéed vegetables. Cook for 1 to 2 minutes. Stir in the sour cream. Heat to serving temperature over low heat; do not boil. Serve over noodles or rice.

Yield: 4 servings

Pat Martin

CRESCENT MOON DESIGN

When William Harvey's translation of Schherazade's enticing tales of the Arabian Nights reached the booksellers of Victorian England, Islamic decoration suddenly became the fashion, although accuracy of ornamentation was not necessarily attempted. The crescent moons topping the hotel's 13 minarets refer to the lunar months of the Moslem calendar.

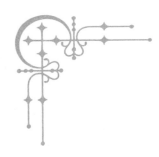

Greek Stifado

2 onions, thinly sliced
1/2 cup butter
3 pounds lean stew beef
Salt and pepper to taste
1 bay leaf
1/2 cup currants
1 (6-ounce) can tomato paste
1 1/2 cups dry red wine

2 tablespoons wine vinegar
1 tablespoon brown sugar
2 large cloves of garlic, crushed
1/2 teaspoon cumin
1/2 teaspoon ground cloves
8 ounces feta cheese
1 cup chopped walnuts

Sauté the onions in the butter in a large skillet. Cut the beef into 1 1/2-inch cubes. Sprinkle with salt and pepper. Add to the skillet and mix until the beef is coated with the onions. Add the bay leaf and currants. Combine the tomato paste, wine, vinegar, brown sugar, garlic, cumin and cloves in a small bowl and mix well. Add to the skillet and mix well. Simmer, covered, for 2 hours or until the meat is very tender, stirring occasionally. Sprinkle with the feta cheese and walnuts. Let the stew stand until the cheese melts. Serve over hot cooked rice.

Yield: 6 servings

Gwen Young

Amusements

After Henry Plant had enticed his guests down to the Tampa Bay Hotel, he felt obliged to offer them a selection of daytime diversions, the town having naught to offer. His staff could arrange an afternoon at the hotel racetrack, a hunting expedition for Florida panther or black bear, as well as bicycle and horseback riding, shuffleboard and billiards, swimming, fishing, tennis, golf and boating from a Japanese pagoda on the riverbank.

Main Dishes

POLISH BIGOS

*This winter comfort food is good with potato pancakes and a
mug of beer. It is excellent reheated.*

3 slices bacon
1 tablespoon margarine
10 to 11 ounces beef chuck, cubed
1¹/₃ cups chopped onions
1¹/₃ cups chopped Granny Smith
apples
²/₃ (10-ounce) can beef broth

1 cup water
1 teaspoon salt
1 cup bite-size chunks carrots
10 to 11 ounces Polish sausage,
cubed
3 cups shredded cabbage

Fry the bacon in a large skillet until brown and crisp; drain, crumble and set aside. Add the
margarine to the bacon drippings. Brown the beef on all sides in the mixture of butter and bacon
drippings. Add the onions and apples and cook until the apples are tender, stirring frequently.
Add the beef broth, water and salt and mix well. Simmer, covered, for 45 minutes. Add the
carrots and sausage. Cook, covered, for 20 minutes. Add the cabbage and bacon.
Simmer, covered, for 10 minutes longer.

Yield: 4 servings

Phyllis Kimbel

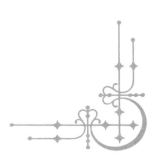

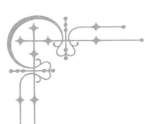

Busy-Day Casserole

8 ounces bacon
1½ pounds ground beef, pork or veal or a mixture
2 teaspoons Worcestershire sauce
Salt and pepper to taste
1 to 2 cups mixed finely chopped celery, shallots, parsley and green bell pepper

2 (4-ounce) cans mushrooms, drained
2 (8-ounce) cans tomato sauce
1 (16-ounce) can green peas
12 ounces noodles, cooked
4 cups shredded Cheddar cheese
¾ cup (about) buttered bread crumbs

Fry the bacon in a large skillet until crisp; drain, reserving a small amount of drippings. Crumble the bacon and set aside. Cook the ground meat in the bacon drippings until brown and crumbly, stirring frequently. Stir in the Worcestershire sauce, salt and pepper. Add the mixed celery, shallots, parsley and green pepper and mix well. Stir in the mushrooms and tomato sauce. Simmer for several minutes. Drain the peas and stir gently into the mixture. Alternate layers of the noodles, meat mixture and cheese in a lightly greased baking dish until all the ingredients are used, ending with the cheese. Sprinkle with the bread crumbs. Bake at 350 degrees for 45 minutes or until golden brown and bubbly.

Yield: 6 servings

Elaine Litschgi

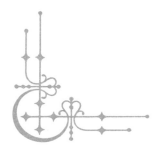

MAURICIO'S MEXICAN PICADILLO

5 pounds lean ground chuck
3 tablespoons olive oil
1 large or 2 medium onions, chopped
1 clove of garlic, crushed
2 (8-ounce) cans tomato sauce
2 jalapeños, finely chopped
1 teaspoon ground cloves
1 teaspoon cinnamon

1/2 cup raisins
1/2 cup chopped pimento-stuffed
  olives
1/4 cup capers
1 apple, peeled, finely chopped
Salt and pepper to taste
1/4 cup sliced almonds, toasted

Cook the ground chuck in the olive oil in a large skillet until brown and crumbly, stirring frequently. Push the ground chuck to the side of the skillet, shaping a well in the center. Sauté the onions and garlic in the center of the skillet until tender. Add the tomato sauce and jalapeños and mix well. Add the cloves, cinnamon, raisins, olives, capers, apple, salt and pepper and mix well. Cook over medium heat for about 20 minutes, stirring frequently. Sprinkle with the toasted almonds. Serve with Spanish yellow rice.

Yield: 10 to 15 servings

Sarah Jane Rubio

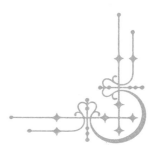

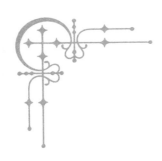

RED'S SPAGHETTI

2 onions, chopped	7 quarts salted water
1/4 cup (about) margarine	78 ounces meat-flavor spaghetti
6 pounds ground round	sauce
24 ounces thin spaghetti	Parmesan cheese to taste

Sauté half the onions in half the margarine in a large skillet until tender. Add half the ground round and cook until brown and crumbly, stirring frequently. Remove the mixture from the skillet to a large dish. Sauté the remaining onions in the remaining margarine in the large skillet until tender. Add the remaining ground round and cook until brown and crumbly, stirring frequently. Remove the mixture from the skillet to a large dish. Break the spaghetti into 1 1/2- to 2-inch pieces. Bring the water to a boil in a large kettle. Add the spaghetti. Cook, uncovered, for 11 minutes, stirring occasionally. Drain the spaghetti in 2 separate colanders. Add one colander of spaghetti to one portion of the ground round mixture. Add 48 ounces of the spaghetti sauce and mix well. Add the remaining colander of spaghetti to the remaining portion of the ground round mixture. Add 30 ounces of the spaghetti sauce and mix well. If you are wondering why the spaghetti has been prepared in this manner, it is because I have no skillet large enough to prepare the entire amount of the sauce at one time. Also, this method allows me to put one portion in the freezer for another day or, better yet, to share with a friend. To prepare to serve the spaghetti, place one or both portions in the same kettle in which the spaghetti was cooked, and heat to serving temperature over low heat, stirring occasionally. Sprinkle servings with Parmesan cheese. Serve with French or Cuban bread. (Recipe written by Red Pittman.)

Yield: 12 servings

Dada Pittman

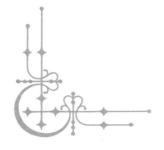

NORTH CAROLINA BARBECUE

I get tired of tomato sauce barbecue. This recipe, from Parker's in Wilson, North Carolina, is a great change and is a quick and easy way to have barbecue.

2 (1-pound) pork tenderloins	2 teaspoons salt
1 tablespoon black pepper	4 slices bacon
1 teaspoon cayenne	Barbecue Sauce

Rub the tenderloins with a mixture of the pepper, cayenne and salt. Wrap 2 bacon slices around each tenderloin and secure with wooden picks or string. Place the tenderloins on a preheated grill. Baste sparingly with Barbecue Sauce. Cook, covered, for 5 minutes. Turn the tenderloins over, baste and cook, covered, for 5 minutes. Repeat the turning, basting and cooking steps twice more. Remove the bacon strips and discard. Slice or shred the tenderloins, moisten with Barbecue Sauce and serve.

Yield: 6 servings

BARBECUE SAUCE

1/2 cup butter	2 tablespoons Worcestershire
1 cup cider vinegar	sauce
1 large sour pickle, minced	1 tablespoon molasses
1 tablespoon minced onion	Salt and pepper to taste
1 tablespoon lemon juice	

Combine the butter, vinegar, pickle, onion, lemon juice, Worcestershire sauce and molasses in a saucepan. Cook over low heat just long enough to melt the butter, stirring frequently. Add the salt and pepper.

Yield: 2 cups

Kathryn Turner

Bob's Memphis-Style Barbecue

Ribs or chicken pieces
Robinson's Rub for Barbecue or
a mixture of seasoned salt, pepper
and garlic powder

2 tablespoons white Worcestershire
sauce
1/2 teaspoon liquid smoke
2 cups apple cider vinegar

Remove the membrane from the underside of the ribs, or rinse the chicken and pat dry. Place in a large pan. Sprinkle the rub generously on all sides and set aside to marinate. Combine 1/4 cup of the rub with the remaining ingredients in a 1-quart measure. Add enough water to fill the measure. Place the ribs or chicken on the rack of a gas grill (use a gas grill only). Grill for 5 minutes on each side. Baste and continue to turn and baste every 10 minutes until dark brown. Do not parboil the ribs. Add barbecue sauce at serving time.

Yield: variable

Pat Wilson

Barbecued Pork Tenderloin

6 pounds pork tenderloins
3 cups chopped peeled apples
2 cups raisins

1 cup chopped celery
1 (16-ounce) bottle barbecue sauce
2 cups packed brown sugar

Place the tenderloins in a shallow roasting pan. Layer the apples, raisins and celery over the top. Pour the barbecue sauce over the layers. Sprinkle with the brown sugar. Bake at 300 degrees for 1 1/2 hours or to 185 degrees on a meat thermometer. Remove to a serving platter. Garnish with unpeeled apple slices and parsley sprigs. Serve with the sauce and wild rice.

Yield: 10 to 12 servings

Freddie Ennis

Bourbon-Baked Pork Tenderloin with Mustard Sauce

*This tenderloin is delicious served for hors d'oeuvre with
small soft rolls, biscuits or bread slices.*

2 (1-pound) pork tenderloins
¼ cup bourbon
2 tablespoons brown sugar
¼ cup soy sauce
Mustard Sauce

Place the tenderloins in a shallow baking pan. Mix the bourbon, brown sugar
and soy sauce in a small bowl. Pour over the tenderloins. Marinate at room temperature for
4 to 6 hours. Bake at 325 degrees for 30 to 40 minutes or until tender, basting
frequently with marinade. Serve with Mustard Sauce.

Yield: 6 to 8 main dish servings or 20 to 30 appetizer servings

Mustard Sauce

⅓ cup sour cream
⅓ cup mayonnaise
1 teaspoon dry mustard
1½ teaspoons vinegar
1 tablespoon finely chopped
green onions

Combine the sour cream, mayonnaise, dry mustard and vinegar in a small
bowl and blend well. Stir in the green onions.

Yield: ¾ cup

Kathryn Turner

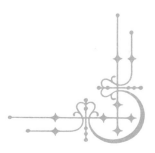

Pork Tenderloin with Raspberry Walnut Vinaigrette

The Raspberry Walnut Vinaigrette served with this is also excellent as a dressing for simple greens.

3 1/2 to 4 pounds pork tenderloins
Zest and juice of 2 oranges
1 cup finely chopped yellow onion
1/4 bunch dill, finely chopped
1 bay leaf

Salt and pepper to taste
1/2 cup Southern Comfort
1/2 cup white wine
Mesclun or other hearty greens
Raspberry Walnut Vinaigrette

Trim the tenderloins of all fat and place in a stainless steel bowl. Combine the orange zest, orange juice, onion, dill, bay leaf, salt and pepper, Southern Comfort and white wine in a bowl and mix well. Pour over the tenderloins, turning to coat. Marinate, covered, in the refrigerator for 24 hours. Drain and place on a rack in a broiler pan. Broil to 145 degrees on a meat thermometer. Chill in the refrigerator. Slice the tenderloins diagonally into thin slices. Arrange the slices on a bed of mesclun. Spoon the Raspberry Walnut Vinaigrette over the top.

Yield: 10 servings

Raspberry Walnut Vinaigrette

1/2 cup fresh raspberries
1/2 cup raspberry vinegar
1/2 cup walnut oil

1/4 cup sugar
Salt and white pepper to taste

Purée and strain the raspberries. Mix with the remaining ingredients in a small bowl. Let stand for 1 hour or longer to allow the flavors to blend.

Yield: 1 1/2 cups

Chef Mark Holmberg, Friend of the Chiselers

Pork Tenderloin Medallions

*Serve this as an appetizer with peach or mango chutney on French bread
or prepare three medallions per person as an entrée with rice and a vegetable.*

2 (1½- to 2-pound) tenderloins
Garlic salt and seasoned
pepper to taste

¼ cup melted butter
1 teaspoon rosemary
1 teaspoon thyme

Sprinkle the tenderloins with garlic salt and seasoned pepper. Place fat side up in a shallow baking dish. Brush with the melted butter. Crush the rosemary and thyme together and sprinkle over the tenderloins. Bake at 375 degrees for 45 minutes. Let stand for several minutes before slicing.

Yield: 10 to 12 servings

Joanne Frazier

Pasta Carbonara

6 slices bacon, chopped
¼ cup butter
2 eggs
1 egg yolk

½ cup heavy cream
Salt and pepper to taste
1 pound spaghetti, cooked
⅓ cup grated Parmesan cheese

Sauté the bacon in the butter in a skillet until brown and crisp. Remove with a slotted spoon and keep warm. Beat the eggs and egg yolk in a bowl. Beat in the cream. Add the salt and pepper. Mix with the hot spaghetti in a large bowl. Sprinkle with the bacon and cheese.
Variation: Substitute cooked sausage, crumbled, for the bacon.

Yield: 4 servings

Sharon Pizzo

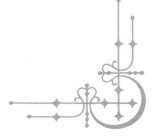

GRILLED BUTTERFLIED LEG OF LAMB

1 (6¹/₂- to 7-pound) leg of lamb
1 cup cider vinegar
3 tablespoons Worcestershire sauce
3 cloves of garlic, mashed into paste
1¹/₂ tablespoons minced fresh mint,
or 1¹/₄ teaspoons dried

2 teaspoons cumin
1 teaspoon pepper
¹/₄ teaspoon Tabasco sauce
Vegetable oil

Have the butcher trim, bone and butterfly the leg of lamb and separate the top round muscle
from the leg to form 2 pieces. Place the lamb in a large glass dish. Combine the vinegar,
Worcestershire sauce, garlic, mint, cumin, pepper and Tabasco sauce in a small bowl and mix well.
Pour the mixture over the lamb. Refrigerate, covered, for 2 to 12 hours, turning
the lamb occasionally. Brush the grill with oil. Drain the lamb, reserving the marinade. Place the
lamb over glowing coals. Grill for 30 to 40 minutes or to 140 degrees on a meat thermometer
for medium-rare, basting occasionally with the reserved marinade and turning once. Place the
lamb on a serving platter. Let stand for 10 minutes. Hold the knife at a 45-degree
angle and slice across the grain into ¹/₄-inch slices.

Yield: 6 to 8 servings

Bertha Nelson, Sherrill O'Neal

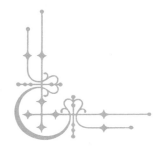

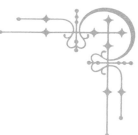

GINGERED LAMB

1 leg of lamb	¼ cup soy sauce
1 large onion	2 tablespoons vegetable oil
1 (1-inch) piece peeled gingerroot	¼ cup honey
1 jalapeño	

Have the butcher trim, bone and butterfly the leg of lamb. Chop the onion, gingerroot and jalapeño. Combine with the soy sauce, oil and honey in a bowl and mix well. Place the lamb in a dish. Pour the onion mixture over the lamb. Marinate, covered, in the refrigerator for 8 to 12 hours, turning several times. Remove the lamb from the marinade; reserve the marinade. Place the lamb on a preheated grill with the boned side up. Grill for 5 to 6 minutes on each side or until seared or lightly charred, basting several times with the reserved marinade. Place the lamb in a baking pan. Keep warm, uncovered, in a 250-degree oven until serving time.

Yield: 6 to 8 servings

Mary Ellen Germany

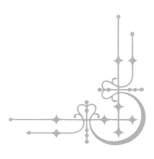

Haggis in a Pan

This authentic dish from Scotland is peasant food at its best. The hulled oats are also called oat groats and can be purchased at any health food store.

4 ounces calves liver
2 onions
8 ounces lean ground beef or lamb
2/3 cup whole hulled oats, or oat groats

3 tablespoons vegetable oil
1 teaspoon salt
1 teaspoon pepper
2 2/3 cups water

Process the liver, onions and ground beef in a food grinder and set aside. Sauté the oats in the oil in a skillet until brown. Add the salt, pepper, water and ground liver mixture and mix well. Spoon the mixture into a greased loaf pan. Bake, covered with foil, at 350 degrees for 1 1/2 hours. Let stand, covered, until cool. Invert the loaf onto a plate and cut into slices. Heat a small amount of additional vegetable oil in a skillet. Add the sliced haggis and fry until brown on both sides. Serve with hot mustard, mashed yellow turnips, crisp bread and fried apples.

Yield: 4 to 6 servings

Phyllis Kimbel

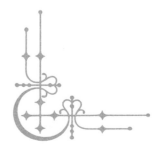

CHICKEN MARENGO

2 cups sliced fresh mushrooms
2 tablespoons butter or margarine
3 pounds chicken legs, thighs
and breasts
Salt and pepper to taste
2 to 3 tablespoons olive oil

4 green onions
1 clove of garlic, crushed
1 cup dry white wine
2 tomatoes, cut into wedges
1/4 teaspoon thyme
1 tablespoon parsley

Sauté the mushrooms in the butter in a skillet for 2 minutes. Set the mushrooms aside. Rinse the chicken and pat dry. Sprinkle the chicken with salt and pepper. Brown the chicken in the olive oil in a large skillet. Remove the chicken and set aside; reserve pan drippings. Remove the green onion tops and slice the green onions. Sauté the green onions and garlic in the pan drippings until tender. Stir in the wine, tomatoes, thyme, salt and pepper, stirring to deglaze the skillet. Arrange the chicken pieces in the skillet. Simmer, covered, for 30 minutes or until the chicken is tender. Add the sautéed mushrooms and sprinkle with the parsley. Serve the chicken with hot cooked rice, spooning the vegetables and pan juices over the rice.

Yield: 6 servings

Dot Cason

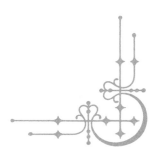

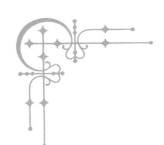

BIRDS OF PARADISE

A lifesaver when you've run out of ideas for dinner.

6 boneless skinless chicken breasts
1 egg
2 tablespoons (about) milk

¾ cup grated Parmesan cheese
¼ cup butter or margarine
¾ cup dry white wine or chicken broth

Rinse the chicken and pat dry. Cut into strips and set aside. Beat the egg with the milk in a medium bowl. Dip the chicken into the egg mixture and roll in the cheese, coating well. Melt the butter in a nonstick skillet. Add the chicken and cook until light brown on all sides. Sprinkle any remaining cheese over the chicken. Add the wine. Simmer, covered, for 35 minutes. Simmer, uncovered, for 10 minutes longer or until the pan juices are reduced to the desired consistency.

Yield: 6 servings

Sallie Holmberg

CRANBERRY CHICKEN

4 to 6 boneless skinless chicken breasts
1 (8-ounce) bottle Russian or Catalina
salad dressing

1 (16-ounce) can whole cranberry
sauce
1 envelope onion soup mix

Rinse the chicken and pat dry. Arrange in a 9x13-inch baking dish sprayed with nonstick cooking spray. Mix the remaining ingredients in a bowl. Spoon over the chicken. Marinate, covered, in the refrigerator for 2 hours or longer. Bake, uncovered, at 350 degrees for 1 to 1½ hours or until the chicken is tender. Serve over hot cooked long grain and wild rice.

Yield: 4 to 6 servings

Monk Brannon

TIPSY CHICKEN

4 large boneless skinless
chicken breasts
2 cups port or sherry
2 tablespoons brandy
Salt and pepper to taste

¼ cup butter, softened
½ teaspoon tarragon vinegar
¼ cup pâté de fois gras
2 tablespoons butter

Rinse the chicken and pat dry. Pound the chicken between waxed paper to flatten.
Place the chicken in a non-metallic bowl. Add the wine and brandy. Marinate in the refrigerator
for 1 hour. Drain, reserving the marinade. Sprinkle the chicken with salt and pepper.
Blend ¼ cup butter with the vinegar in a small bowl. Spread 1 tablespoon of the butter mixture
and 1 tablespoon of the pâté over each chicken breast; fold the chicken over to enclose
the filling and secure with string. Brown the chicken in 2 tablespoons butter in a large skillet.
Pour the reserved marinade over the chicken. Simmer, uncovered, for 30 minutes or
until the chicken is tender, basting occasionally with the pan drippings. Remove the string
carefully and place the chicken on a serving platter. Boil the pan drippings for several
minutes to reduce to the desired consistency and spoon over the chicken.

Yield: 2 to 4 servings

Lynne Smith

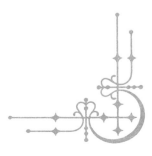

MOTHER'S CHICKEN CASSEROLE

8 boneless skinless chicken breasts
Chicken broth
2 (10-ounce) cans cream of
chicken soup

2 cups sour cream
1 tablespoon lemon juice
2 stacks saltine crackers, crushed
1 cup melted butter

Rinse the chicken and place in a large saucepan. Add enough broth to cover. Cook over medium heat until tender. Drain, reserving the broth. Cool the chicken and cut into bite-size pieces. Mix the soup, sour cream and lemon juice in a bowl. Stir in 1/2 cup of the broth. Mix the cracker crumbs with the butter in a bowl. Layer half the crumbs, the chicken, the soup mixture and the remaining crumbs in a 9x13-inch baking dish. Bake at 350 degrees for 1 hour or until brown.

Yield: 8 servings

Sue House

CHICKEN AND WILD RICE CASSEROLE

1 (10-ounce) package frozen broccoli
1 (7-ounce) package long grain and wild
rice mix, cooked
4 boneless skinless chicken breasts,
cooked, chopped

1 (10-ounce) can cream of
mushroom soup
1 cup mayonnaise
1 cup (about) bread crumbs
Shredded Cheddar cheese to taste

Cook the broccoli using the package directions and drain. Layer the rice, chicken and broccoli in a 9x13-inch baking dish. Mix the soup and mayonnaise in a bowl. Spoon over the broccoli. Sprinkle with the crumbs and cheese. Bake at 350 degrees for 40 minutes or until brown.

Yield: 6 to 8 servings

Nadyne Hines

Coq au Vin Rouge

2 pounds boneless skinless chicken
breasts and thighs
1/2 cup flour
1/4 teaspoon salt
1/4 teaspoon paprika
Pepper to taste
1/4 cup shortening or vegetable oil
10 small whole onions
1/4 cup chopped celery with leaves

1 clove of garlic, minced
1/8 teaspoon thyme
1/8 teaspoon rosemary
1 bay leaf
1 (10-ounce) can chicken consommé
1/4 cup burgundy
1 (4-ounce) can mushrooms, drained
2 tablespoons parsley

Rinse the chicken and pat dry. Dust the chicken with a mixture of the flour, salt, paprika and pepper. Reserve any remaining flour mixture. Brown the chicken on all sides in the hot shortening in a large skillet. Remove the chicken and pour off almost all of the drippings. Add the onions, celery, garlic, thyme, rosemary and bay leaf to the skillet. Sauté for several minutes. Add the reserved flour mixture and mix well. Stir the consommé and wine into the skillet and arrange the chicken pieces in the mixture. Cook, covered, over low heat for 45 minutes, stirring occasionally. Add the mushrooms and parsley. Cook, covered, for several minutes longer or until the sauce is of the desired consistency.

Yield: 4 to 6 servings

Helen Martin

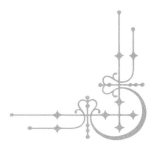

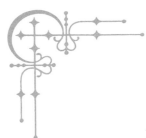

Drunken Drumsticks

8 plump chicken legs	1/4 teaspoon pepper
1 cup full-bodied red wine	2 tablespoons dark brown sugar
2 tablespoons wine vinegar	1 teaspoon Worcestershire sauce
1/2 teaspoon salt	1/2 cup catsup
1/2 teaspoon garlic salt	2 tablespoons butter

Rinse the chicken and pat dry. Place the chicken in a shallow dish. Combine the wine, vinegar, salt, garlic salt and pepper in a small bowl and mix well. Pour over the chicken. Marinate, covered, in the refrigerator for 8 to 12 hours. Drain the chicken, reserving the marinade. Add the brown sugar, Worcestershire sauce and catsup to the reserved marinade and mix well. Heat the butter in a large skillet. Add the chicken and cook until light brown on all sides. Add the brown sugar mixture. Cook, covered, over medium-low heat for 40 minutes or until the chicken is tender, turning often. Serve with hot cooked rice.

Yield: 8 servings

Betty Culbreath

Waltz Time

In the evenings they danced, swirling across the polished ballroom floor or waltzing through the ring of French doors onto the veranda, wide as a country road. Thirteen gold crescent moons glowed overhead, one atop each minaret rising high above the roofline. And on some nights an even brighter silver moon paved a trembling pathway over the river.

Main Dishes

Savory Chicken-in-a-Crust

<table>
<tr><td>1/2 cup sliced carrots</td><td>1/2 cup sliced mushrooms</td></tr>
<tr><td>1/2 cup chopped onion</td><td>1 (10-ounce) can cream of</td></tr>
<tr><td>1/2 cup chopped celery</td><td>chicken soup</td></tr>
<tr><td>2 tablespoons butter</td><td>Salt and pepper to taste</td></tr>
<tr><td>1/2 cup chopped pimentos</td><td>Sour Cream and Thyme Pastry</td></tr>
<tr><td>2 cups chopped cooked chicken</td><td>1 cup shredded sharp Cheddar</td></tr>
<tr><td>or turkey</td><td>cheese</td></tr>
</table>

Sauté the carrots, onion and celery in the butter in a large skillet for several minutes. Add the pimentos, chicken and mushrooms. Add the soup, salt and pepper and mix well. Spoon into the Sour Cream and Thyme Pastry. Sprinkle with the cheese. Bake at 400 degrees for 30 minutes.

Sour Cream and Thyme Pastry

<table>
<tr><td>1/2 cup butter, softened</td><td>1 teaspoon salt</td></tr>
<tr><td>1 cup sour cream</td><td>1 teaspoon baking powder</td></tr>
<tr><td>1 egg</td><td>1/2 to 1 teaspoon thyme</td></tr>
<tr><td>1 cup flour</td><td></td></tr>
</table>

Cream the butter and sour cream in a medium bowl. Add the egg and mix well. Mix the flour with salt, baking powder and thyme. Add to the sour cream mixture and mix well. Spread the mixture evenly over the bottom and up the sides of a greased 9x13-inch baking dish.

Yield: 6 to 8 servings

Ruth Turbeville

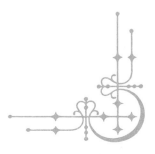

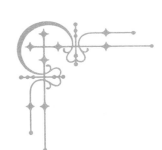

Chicken Jerusalem

1 (3-pound) chicken	$^1/_3$ to $^1/_2$ cup dry sherry
Salt and pepper to taste	1 tablespoon lemon juice
2 tablespoons (or more) butter	1 cup cream
4 artichoke hearts	$1^1/_2$ tablespoons chopped chives
1 (4-ounce) can sliced mushrooms	$^3/_4$ cup sour cream

Cut the chicken into serving pieces. Rinse the chicken and pat dry. Sprinkle with salt and pepper. Cook the chicken pieces in the butter in a large skillet until tender and brown on all sides. Cut the artichoke hearts into halves. Add the artichokes and mushrooms to the skillet and mix well. Add the sherry and lemon juice and cook until the liquid is reduced. Add the cream and chives and mix well. Cook for about 5 minutes, stirring occasionally. Remove the chicken to a warm platter. Whisk the sour cream into the sauce. Spoon the sauce over the chicken.

Yield: 4 to 6 servings

Betty Culbreath

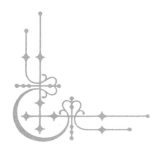

REALLY GOOD CHICKEN AND ASPARAGUS

2 cups (or more) chopped cooked
chicken
2 cups cooked rice
1/2 cup chopped pimentos
1 cup chopped almonds

1 cup mayonnaise
1 (15-ounce) can asparagus, drained,
chopped
Salt, pepper and garlic salt to taste
Tabasco sauce to taste

Combine the chicken, rice, pimentos and almonds in a bowl and mix well. Add the mayonnaise
and mix well. Add the asparagus and mix gently. Season with salt, pepper, garlic salt and
Tabasco sauce. Spoon into a 3-quart casserole. Bake at 300 degrees for 30 minutes.

Yield: 12 servings

Mary Anderson

MARINATED TURKEY

1 turkey
1 small clove of garlic, crushed,
and 1/2 teaspoon dried oregano
per pound of turkey

1 teaspoon salt
1 teaspoon olive oil
1/2 teaspoon vinegar
Pepper to taste

Rinse the turkey inside and out and pat dry. Mix the remaining ingredients in a small bowl. Rub
the mixture over the inside and outside of the turkey. Use the entire amount of the prepared
mixture. Wrap the turkey tightly in foil. Refrigerate overnight. Unwrap the turkey. Place in a
roasting pan. Roast at 325 degrees for 20 to 25 minutes per pound or to 180 to 185 degrees on a
meat thermometer, basting occasionally. Let stand for 15 to 30 minutes before carving.

Yield: variable

Louise Jackson

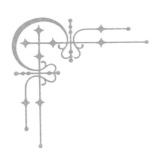

DUCK CREOLE

2 ducks   2 tablespoons (about)
Salt to taste   vegetable oil
1/2 apple   Bacon slices
1 onion   Creole Sauce
Celery to taste   Flour
Pepper to taste

Rinse the ducks inside and out and place in a large kettle. Add water to cover and bring to a boil. Parboil for 10 minutes and drain well. Sprinkle the cavities with salt. Cut the apple, onion and celery into pieces and stuff the ducks. Rub the ducks with a mixture of salt, pepper and vegetable oil. Place the ducks breast side down in a roasting pan. Arrange bacon slices over ducks and cover with Creole Sauce. Bake, covered, at 300 degrees for 2 hours or until the ducks are tender. Remove the ducks to a serving platter. Blend a small amount of flour with a small amount of cold water. Stir into the pan juices and cook until thickened, stirring constantly. Remove and discard the bay leaves. Serve the gravy with the ducks.

CREOLE SAUCE

1/2 cup butter   1 (16-ounce) can tomatoes,
1 onion, chopped   chopped
2 bay leaves   Salt and pepper to taste

Combine the butter, onion, bay leaves, undrained tomatoes, salt and pepper in a saucepan. Bring to a boil and reduce the heat. Simmer for 30 minutes, stirring occasionally.

Yield: 4 servings

Lora Hulse

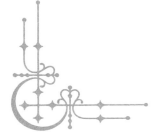

GROUPER MEDITERRANEAN

¹/₂ cup chopped onion

1 tablespoon minced garlic

2 tablespoons olive oil

¹/₂ cup dry white wine

3 cups crushed tomatoes

¹/₄ cup drained capers

¹/₂ teaspoon rosemary

¹/₂ teaspoon oregano

¹/₄ teaspoon red pepper flakes

¹/₂ cup chopped fresh parsley

1 tablespoon olive oil

3 pounds grouper fillets, at room temperature

2 tablespoons sambuca

8 ounces feta cheese

Sauté the onion and garlic in 2 tablespoons olive oil in a large skillet for several minutes. Do not allow the garlic to brown. Add the wine, tomatoes, capers, rosemary , oregano, pepper flakes and parsley and mix well. Simmer for 10 minutes. Pour 1 tablespoon olive oil into a shallow baking dish, tilting to coat the bottom. Cut the grouper into 6 portions and arrange in a single layer in the baking dish. Spoon the sauce over the grouper. Bake at 450 degrees for 15 minutes. Preheat the broiler. Sprinkle the sambuca and feta cheese over the grouper. Broil until the cheese is light brown and begins to melt.

Yield: 6 servings

Doris Harvey

WISH YOU WERE HERE

A guest described the Hotel's lobby "cozy as a family sitting room. Everything that is going on may be watched from the rocking chairs and arm chairs that dot the floor. . . . There are scores of these chairs, many bronze statues, handsome paintings . . . open fireplaces and big antique vases that are uncommon handy to drop cigar ashes in. . . ."

MAIN DISHES

Fillet of Redfish

Gladys, who cooked for my family for 39 years, brought this recipe with her.

1/2 cup butter
6 pounds redfish or red snapper fillets
Juice of 1 lemon

Parmesan cheese to taste
Salt and pepper to taste

Broil the butter in a broiler pan until brown (this is the secret of the good flavor). Arrange the fillets skin side up in the butter. Broil for 10 minutes. Turn the fillets over carefully. Sprinkle with lemon juice, Parmesan cheese, salt and pepper. Baste with the pan drippings. Broil for 10 minutes longer. Do not use margarine in this recipe.

Yield: 4 servings

Eloise Brooker

Sidecar Salmon

2 cups chopped red onions
2 tablespoons olive oil

4 salmon fillets
1/2 cup reduced-sodium soy sauce

Sauté the onions in the olive oil in a large skillet until translucent. Arrange the salmon fillets over the onions. Drizzle the soy sauce over the fillets. Cook, covered, over low heat for 10 to 12 minutes or until the salmon is opaque. Remove the salmon to a serving platter and keep warm. Cook the onions until brown and caramelized. Serve the onions with the salmon.

Yield: 4 servings

Mary Baker Robbins

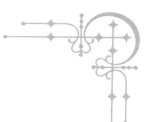

TAMPA BAY FISH BAKE

1 tablespoon vegetable oil
2 onions, thinly sliced
2 pounds fish fillets
1 1/2 teaspoons salt
1/4 teaspoon nutmeg
1/4 teaspoon black pepper
1/2 teaspoon cayenne

2 large tomatoes, sliced
1 (3-ounce) can sliced mushrooms
1 teaspoon Kitchen Bouquet
1/4 cup sherry or white wine
Seasoned bread crumbs

Pour the oil into a baking dish and tilt to coat the bottom. Cover the bottom of the baking dish with onion slices. Arrange a layer of fillets over the onions and sprinkle with a mixture of salt, nutmeg, pepper and cayenne. Arrange a layer of tomato slices over the fillets. Combine the undrained mushrooms, Kitchen Bouquet and sherry in a small bowl and mix well. Spoon over the layers. Bake at 350 degrees for 15 minutes. Sprinkle the bread crumbs over the top. Bake for 15 minutes longer or until the fish flakes easily.

Yield: 4 to 6 servings

Clarajo Hurley

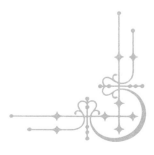

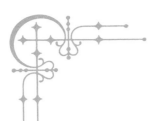

BAYSHORE DEVILED CRAB

1/4 cup fresh lemon juice

2 teaspoons prepared mustard

2 tablespoons Worcestershire sauce

1/2 teaspoon salt

1/2 teaspoon pepper

1 clove of garlic, crushed

1 pound fresh crab claw meat

6 tablespoons melted butter

2 tablespoons milk

2 tablespoons white wine

1 stack butter crackers,
   very finely crushed

8 teaspoons butter

8 thin lemon slices

Combine the lemon juice, mustard, Worcestershire sauce, salt, pepper and garlic in a small bowl and mix well. Place the crab meat in a large bowl, discarding the shells. Add the lemon juice mixture, melted butter, milk, wine and 3/4 of the cracker crumbs to the crab meat and mix well. Add additional cracker crumbs if the mixture is too soupy or a bit of additional milk if too dry. Spoon the mixture into baking shells or ramekins. Sprinkle with the remaining cracker crumbs and press in lightly. Top each shell with a teaspoon of butter and a lemon slice. Bake at 350 degrees for 30 minutes or until the cracker crumbs are golden brown.

Yield: 8 servings

Mary Ruth Hodges

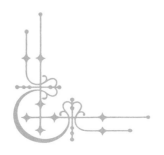

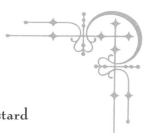

CRAB MEAT IMPERIAL

¹/₄ cup chopped green bell pepper

¹/₄ cup chopped celery

1 (2-ounce) jar chopped pimento, drained

2 tablespoons butter

1 tablespoon chopped fresh parsley

1 teaspoon Old Bay seasoning

¹/₂ teaspoon prepared mustard

Hot sauce to taste

Red pepper flakes to taste

1 egg, beaten

3 tablespoons mayonnaise

1 pound fresh lump crab meat

Sauté the green pepper, celery and pimento in the butter in a skillet until tender. Add the parsley, Old Bay seasoning, mustard, hot sauce and pepper flakes and mix well. Blend the egg and mayonnaise in a large bowl. Stir in the sautéed vegetables. Add the crab meat and mix gently. Spoon into baking shells or ramekins. Bake at 375 degrees for 15 minutes. Broil for 2 to 3 minutes. Garnish with pimento strips and celery leaves.

Yield: 4 servings

Libby Dickinson

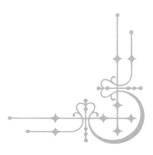

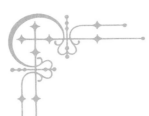

CRAB DELIGHT

1 small onion, chopped
1/4 cup chopped green bell pepper
3 tablespoons butter
3 tablespoons flour
1 1/2 cups milk
1 teaspoon salt
1/2 teaspoon pepper
1/2 teaspoon Worcestershire sauce

2 tablespoons lemon juice
Curry powder to taste
Dry mustard to taste
1 (14-ounce) can artichokes, drained
2 cups crab meat
4 hard-cooked eggs, chopped
1/4 cup grated Parmesan cheese

Sauté the onion and green pepper in the butter in a skillet until tender. Mix in the flour. Add the milk gradually, stirring constantly. Cook until thickened, stirring constantly. Add the salt, pepper, Worcestershire sauce, lemon juice, curry powder and dry mustard and mix well. Remove from the heat. Cut the artichokes into bite-size pieces and place in a bowl. Add the crab meat, eggs and sauce and mix well. Spoon into a 2-quart casserole, or individual baking shells or ramekins. Sprinkle with Parmesan cheese. Bake at 350 degrees for 30 minutes.

Yield: 4 to 6 servings

Margaret Davis

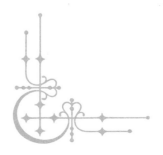

WILD RICE AND OYSTER CASSEROLE

3 cups long grain and wild
rice mix
1/2 cup chopped onion
2 cups chopped celery
1/4 cup butter
3 tablespoons flour
1/2 cup milk

1/2 teaspoon salt
1/4 teaspoon sage
1/8 teaspoon pepper
1 pint oysters
1/2 cup melted butter
Cracker crumbs

Cook the rice mix using the package directions and set aside. Sauté the onion and celery in 1/4 cup butter in a skillet until tender. Remove from the heat and add the flour, mixing well. Stir in the milk, salt, sage and pepper. Add the rice and mix well. Pour into a greased 2-quart casserole. Drain the oysters and add to 1/2 cup butter in a bowl. Let stand for 5 to 10 minutes. Pour over the rice mixture, arranging the oysters evenly over the rice. Sprinkle with cracker crumbs. Bake at 350 degrees for 45 minutes.

Yield: 8 servings

Betty Wood

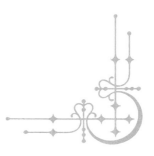

LOBSTER WITH BRANDY CREAM

1 small sweet onion, chopped
1/4 cup butter
8 ounces fresh mushrooms, sliced
4 or 5 tomatoes, peeled, seeded, chopped
3 cups coarsely chopped cooked lobster

2 cups heavy cream
Salt and pepper to taste
Tabasco sauce to taste
3 or 4 drops of bitters
1/4 cup brandy
1 cup chopped parsley
3 cups hot cooked rice

Sauté the onion in the butter in a large skillet until tender. Add the mushrooms and sauté for 5 minutes. Add the tomatoes and cook until the tomato juices are released. Add the lobster and cream and mix well. Cook just until the mixture begins to simmer. Add the salt, pepper, Tabasco sauce, bitters and brandy. Fold in the parsley. Chill for up to 12 hours at this point if desired. Spread the rice over the bottom of a baking dish. Spoon the lobster mixture over the top. Bake at 350 degrees for 30 minutes.

Yield: 6 servings

Betty B. Farrior

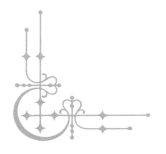

Cheesy Crab and Shrimp Casserole

8 ounces cream cheese
1/2 cup margarine
1 pound peeled shrimp
1 medium onion, chopped
1 medium green bell pepper, chopped
2 tablespoons margarine
1 (10-ounce) can cream of mushroom soup

1 (8-ounce) can sliced mushrooms
1 teaspoon Tabasco sauce
1/2 teaspoon red pepper flakes
2 cups crab meat
3/4 cup uncooked rice
1 cup shredded sharp Cheddar cheese
1 cup (about) cracker crumbs

Heat the cream cheese and 1/2 cup margarine in a large saucepan over low heat until melted, stirring frequently; set aside. Sauté the shrimp, onion and green pepper in 2 tablespoons margarine in a skillet until the onion is translucent and the shrimp just turn pink. Mix the shrimp mixture with the melted cream cheese mixture. Add the soup, mushrooms, Tabasco sauce, pepper flakes, crab meat and rice. Place in a greased 2-quart casserole. Top with the cheese and cracker crumbs. Bake at 350 degrees for 30 minutes or until the rice is tender.

Yield: 8 servings

Anne Cloar

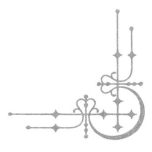

SCALLOPED SHRIMP AND CRAB MEAT

½ cup finely chopped celery
Finely chopped fresh parsley to taste
1 pound fresh crab meat or 2 small cans
8 ounces shrimp, cooked, peeled
3 hard-cooked eggs, chopped

Chopped pimento to taste
1 to 2 cups white sauce prepared with
  half-and-half
Soft bread crumbs
Butter

Combine the celery, parsley, crab meat, shrimp, eggs and pimento in a bowl. Add enough white sauce to make the mixture of the desired consistency. Spoon into a greased baking dish. Sprinkle with bread crumbs and dot with butter. Bake at 400 degrees for 20 to 25 minutes or just until bubbly.

Yield: 4 to 6 servings

Camille McWhirter

SHRIMP NEWBURG

1½ pounds shrimp, peeled, deveined
⅔ cup each chopped onion and celery
⅔ chopped green bell pepper (optional)
⅔ cup butter
1⅓ cups evaporated milk

2 (10-ounce) cans cream of potato soup
1 drop of red food coloring
1 cup shredded sharp Cheddar cheese
2 tablespoons lemon juice
2 tablespoons sherry (optional)

Boil the shrimp just until pink; drain. Sauté the onion, celery and green pepper in the butter in a skillet until tender. Stir in the evaporated milk, soup, food coloring, cheese, lemon juice, sherry and shrimp. Heat to serving temperature. Serve over rice or toast points, or in patty shells.

Yield: 6 to 8 servings

Olliff Smith

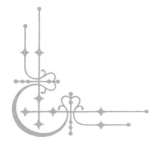

EASY CAJUN SHRIMP

8 ears corn

4 to 5 pounds large unpeeled shrimp

1/4 cup olive oil

1/4 cup Worcestershire sauce

1/4 cup soy sauce

2 teaspoons salt

2 teaspoons pepper

2 cloves of garlic, crushed

2 tablespoons dried oregano

Cayenne to taste

1/2 teaspoon Tabasco sauce, or to taste

1 cup butter

4 lemons, sliced

Cook the corn in boiling water to cover for 5 minutes; drain. Cut the ears into halves. Place the corn and shrimp in a large deep roaster. Mix the olive oil, Worcestershire sauce, soy sauce, salt, pepper, garlic, oregano, cayenne and Tabasco sauce in a small bowl. Drizzle over the corn and shrimp. Dot with butter. Top with the lemon slices. Bake at 500 degrees for 8 to 10 minutes or until the shrimp turn pink, basting with the pan juices.

Yield: 8 servings

Judy More

PARASOLS AND PETTICOATS

The Tampa Bay Hotel's ornamental gardens were adorned with fountains, peacocks, palm trees and porcelain garden seats from China. The little barrel-shaped stools, painted with blossoms and butterflies, were as practical as they were decorative, and most gratefully sought after by the ladies, whose tightly laced corsets and waist cinchers allowed for no more than distressingly shallow breaths of air.

MAIN DISHES

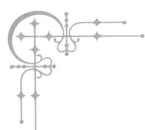

TRINIDAD SHRIMP CURRY

1 coconut

2 large onions, chopped

Crushed garlic to taste

1/4 cup vegetable oil

2 large tomatoes, chopped

2 tablespoons (or more) curry powder

1 tablespoon shredded coconut

2 1/2 pounds uncooked peeled shrimp

2 apples, chopped

2 potatoes, scrubbed, chopped

Salt and pepper to taste

Worcestershire sauce to taste

Hot cooked patna rice

Chutney

Grated peanuts

Slivered almonds

Grated coconut

Chopped hard-cooked egg yolks

Chopped hard-cooked egg whites

Crumbled crisp-cooked bacon

Drain and reserve the liquid from the coconut. Grate the coconut and add to the reserved liquid. Let the mixture stand in a warm place to steep. Pour the mixture into a clean heavy cloth in a colander or strainer and reserve both the liquid and the coconut. Squeeze the cloth to obtain all the coconut milk possible. Place the grated coconut in a bowl. Add boiling water to cover and let stand to steep. Drain and squeeze, reserving the coconut water. Combine the coconut milk and coconut water to use in the curry. Sauté the onions and garlic in the oil in a large skillet for 5 minutes or just until golden brown. Add the tomatoes. Cook for 2 minutes. Mix the curry powder with 1 cup of the coconut liquid and add to the skillet. Add 1 tablespoon shredded coconut, shrimp, apples and potatoes. Add the salt, pepper and Worcestershire sauce. Simmer for 20 minutes; do not allow the mixture to boil and do not overcook or the apples and potatoes will be mushy. Serve over the rice. Serve the remaining ingredients in separate bowls for garnishing servings to individual tastes.

Yield: 8 servings

A favorite recipe of Chiseler Charter Member Bertha Fletcher, who received it from a friend in Trinidad.

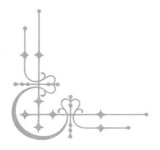

St. Francis Cioppino

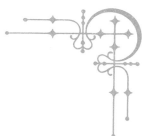

Vince makes this delicious dish every Christmas Eve.

4 medium onions, chopped

6 cloves of garlic, crushed

1/3 cup finely chopped carrot

1/3 cup finely chopped celery

1/3 cup finely chopped leeks

1/2 cup olive oil

1 cup tomato purée

1/2 teaspoon saffron

Legs and body meat of 2 dungeness crabs

8 ounces uncooked shrimp, peeled, deveined

8 ounces scallops, shelled

32 cherrystone clams in shells, scrubbed

32 fresh mussels, scrubbed, beards removed

2 (8-ounce) red snapper fillets, cut into 1-inch pieces

1 (8-ounce) sea bass fillet, cut into 1-inch pieces

8 ounces red snapper fillets, cut into 1-inch pieces

3 cups clam juice

2 cups dry white wine

4 tomatoes, peeled, chopped

1/2 teaspoon thyme

1/2 teaspoon oregano

2 bay leaves

Salt and pepper to taste

1/2 cup parsley

Sauté the onions, garlic, carrot, celery and leeks in the olive oil in a large kettle. Add the tomato purée, saffron and seafood and mix well. Cook for about 2 minutes. Add the clam juice, wine, tomatoes, thyme, oregano, bay leaves, salt and pepper. Simmer for 10 to 15 minutes or until the fish is cooked through. Remove the fish with a slotted spoon and set aside to keep warm. Simmer the fish stock for 10 to 15 minutes or until the juices have reduced slightly. Return the fish to the kettle and bring the mixture to a boil. Remove the bay leaves. Ladle the cioppino into soup bowls and sprinkle with the parsley. Serve with French sourdough bread rubbed with fresh garlic and melted butter and a dish of freshly cooked linguini.

Yield: 8 servings

Lenda Naimoli

Main Dishes

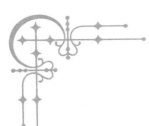

JAMBALAYA

1 medium onion, chopped	2 cups chicken broth
1 small green bell pepper, chopped	2 tablespoons tomato paste
2 tablespoons olive oil	Tabasco sauce to taste
1 teaspoon salt	1 to 2 cups mixed cooked peeled
1 cup uncooked white rice	shrimp and smoked sausage pieces

Sauté the onion and green pepper in the olive oil in a skillet. Add the salt and rice and stir until the rice is coated. Combine the broth, tomato paste and Tabasco sauce in the top of a double boiler. Bring the mixture to a boil over direct heat and stir in the rice mixture. Return to a boil, cover tightly and place the top of the double boiler over the bottom filled with boiling water. Cook for 30 to 40 minutes; do not uncover the rice but do check the bottom of the double boiler to be sure the water does not boil dry. Turn off the heat and let stand for 2 to 4 hours. Add the shrimp and sausage just before serving and reheat to serving temperature over boiling water.

Yield: 4 servings

Jackie O'Connor

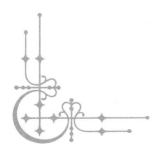

EGGPLANT QUESADILLAS

Borrowed from my friend Sandy Touchton!

1 medium eggplant
1/2 cup chopped onion
1/2 cup sliced mushrooms
1/2 teaspoon salt

1/4 teaspoon pepper
1/2 teaspoon hot pepper sauce
1 1/2 cups shredded mozzarella cheese
4 (8-inch) flour tortillas

Peel the eggplant and cut into 1/4-inch slices. Spray a baking sheet with olive oil cooking spray and arrange the eggplant slices in a single layer on the baking sheet. Broil for 3 to 5 minutes or until brown. Turn the slices over and broil for 3 to 5 minutes. Spray a nonstick skillet with olive oil cooking spray. Add the onion, mushrooms, salt, pepper and hot sauce and sauté until the onion is transparent. Sprinkle 1/4 cup of the cheese onto a tortilla. Add half the sautéed vegetables, half the eggplant, 1/4 cup cheese and another tortilla. Heat a skillet sprayed with olive oil cooking spray over medium-high heat. Place the quesadilla in the skillet. Cook for 2 minutes and turn the quesdilla over. Top with 1/4 cup cheese and cook for 2 minutes longer. Repeat with the remaining tortillas, vegetables and cheese. Serve with salsa and low-fat sour cream.

Yield: 2 servings

Taylor Ikin

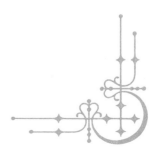

BREADS
&
BRUNCH

*Plant's railroad
delivers guests
to the doors of the
luxury resort.*

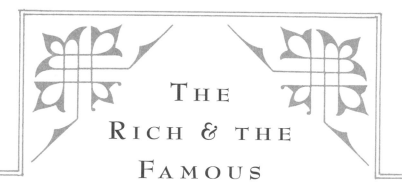

THE RICH & THE FAMOUS

The Tampa Bay Hotel attracted them all, the brilliant, the honored, the popular,
though when Babe Ruth arrived he had not as yet earned his niche in history.
But it was here in the elegant lobby that the Babe signed his first baseball contract
as a pitcher for the Boston Red Sox. And it was here that Stephen Crane,
author of *The Red Badge of Courage*, was inspired to write. And to the hotel came Gloria
Swanson and Nellie Melba, Clara Barton and Teddy Roosevelt, William Jennings Bryan,
Booker T. Washington and Mrs. Ulysses S. Grant. And so many others, blessed by fleeting fame,
whose distinguished names no longer ring familiar. At one time, there were three major generals
of equal rank, doubtlessly a protocol nightmare for the staff. Another day twenty millionaires
were observed taking their ease in the rotunda. The Casino on the hotel grounds lured New York
artists on their way to performances in Cuba. Celebrated actor John Drew took the stage and signed
the hotel register. Anna Pavlova danced and Paderewski played. Sarah Bernhardt, however,
pausing to bestow upon her fans yet another Farewell Performance, refused to sleep in the hotel.
Certain the rooms would be drafty, Sarah preferred to stay in her private railroad car.
The Casino's sumptuous theatre could seat 2,000 on its handsome opera chairs.
Daytime, the floor would be whisked away to reveal a seventy-foot white-tiled
heated bathing pool, with swim instructor and
lady's maid in constant attendance.
No wonder the guests stayed for
weeks at a time!

CHISELSTIX

This recipe was created especially for—and named after—the Chiselers. The Chiselstix are served at most Chiseler functions and much enjoyed by all.

2 pounds bread flour
1/2 ounce sugar
1/2 ounce salt
1/2 ounce dry yeast
8 ounces grated Parmesan cheese
1 tablespoon paprika

1 1/2 teaspoons garlic powder
1/2 teaspoon cayenne
2 ounces freeze-dried chopped chives
1 ounce shortening
2 cups warm water

Combine the flour, sugar, salt and yeast in a large mixer bowl. Add the Parmesan cheese, paprika, garlic powder, cayenne and chives. Add the shortening and warm water. Fit a heavy-duty electric mixer with dough hooks. Beat at low speed with the dough hooks until the mixture is well mixed. Beat on the second speed for 10 to 15 minutes or until the dough is smooth and elastic. Turn the dough onto a lightly floured surface and shape into a ball. Divide into smaller portions for easier handling. Roll each portion into a rectangle 1/4 inch thick and 7 inches wide. Cut into 1/4-inch strips with a sharp knife. Twist each strip and place on greased baking sheets about 1 1/2 inches apart. Let rise in a warm place until doubled in bulk. Bake at 300 degrees for 15 minutes or until brown and crisp. Remove to wire racks to cool.

Yield: 100 Chiselstix

Paul Sparks, Director of Catering

and

Bob Paige, Classic Fare Caterers,
ARAMARK

Cheese Scones

3 cups self-rising flour	1 cup shredded sharp Cheddar
1¼ teaspoons baking powder	cheese
1¼ teaspoons dry mustard	1 egg
⅛ teaspoon salt	1 cup milk

Sift the flour into a large bowl. Add the baking powder, dry mustard and salt and mix well. Stir in the cheese. Beat the egg and milk in a small bowl. Add to the cheese mixture and mix until a soft dough forms. Knead lightly for 1 minute. Pat 1 inch thick on a lightly floured surface. Cut into 2-inch rounds or triangles. Arrange on a lightly greased baking sheet. Bake at 425 degrees for 15 minutes or until light golden brown; do not open the oven while baking. Serve the scones warm with butter, jam or Devonshire cream.

Yield: 12 to 15 scones

Cynthia Gandee, Director, The Henry B. Plant Museum

THE OPEN PETAL ROSETTE DESIGN

An interest in botany flourished in the late 19th century and plant forms became characteristic of decoration, particularly those representing the ideal in nature. Appropriately for a resort hotel, the open petal rosette carved on the Grand Entry door frame symbolized joyous dreams.

Frozen Southern Biscuits

3 cups sifted self-rising flour

½ cup plus 1 tablespoon shortening

½ cup milk

½ cup buttermilk

Place the flour in a bowl. Cut in the shortening until crumbly. Add the milk and buttermilk and mix until moistened. Knead several times on a floured pastry cloth until the dough is smooth. Roll to the desired thickness and cut with a floured biscuit cutter. Arrange on a lightly greased baking sheet. Bake at 400 degrees for 7 minutes or just until slightly colored on top. Let stand until cool. Store, tightly wrapped, in the freezer until needed. Arrange the frozen biscuits on a baking sheet. Bake at 500 degrees for 5 minutes or until brown and serve piping hot.

Yield: 24 biscuits

Dot Compton

Fruitful Muffins

1 cup quick-cooking or rolled oats

1 cup flour

1 tablespoon baking powder

½ teaspoon cinnamon

1 cup skim milk

½ cup mashed banana

½ cup raisins, apricots or dates

¼ cup vegetable oil

¼ cup packed brown sugar

1 egg white, lightly beaten

Combine the oats, flour, baking powder and cinnamon in a medium bowl and mix well. Combine the milk, banana, raisins, oil and brown sugar in a bowl and mix well. Add the egg white and mix well. Add to the oats mixture and mix just until moistened. Fill paper-lined muffin cups ¾ full. Bake at 400 degrees for 20 to 25 minutes or until golden brown.

Yield: 12 muffins

Cynthia Gandee, Director, The Henry B. Plant Museum

Cinnamon Twists

The coveted recipe of the late Lera Farrior.

1 recipe refrigerator roll dough	1 cup sugar
or 1 package frozen dough for rolls	1 cup packed brown sugar
2 cups melted butter	1/3 cup ground cinnamon

Prepare the roll dough or thaw the frozen dough. Let the dough rise according to the recipe or the package directions. Roll 1/4 inch thick on a lightly floured surface. Cut into 1x4-inch strips. Pour enough butter into two 8x10-inch baking pans to cover the bottoms. Mix the sugar, brown sugar and cinnamon in a shallow dish. Dip each dough strip in the melted butter, coat with the cinnamon-sugar mixture. Place a coated strip in a baking pan. Place one finger in the center of the strip, fold the ends over to cross and press lightly to secure. Repeat the process with the remaining strips. Spoon the remaining butter over the twists and sprinkle with the remaining cinnamon-sugar. Bake at 300 degrees for 30 to 45 minutes or until golden brown.

Yield: 2 to 3 dozen

Mary Lee Farrior

Sugar? Lemon?

The gently bred from up North took winter holiday at the magnificent Tampa Bay Hotel and surely Mrs. Potter Palmer could not be outshone in the etiquette of her deportment, the elegance of her ways. As wife of the owner of the world-famous Palmer House, her social activities from matinée to soirée were reported in detail by The Chicago Tribune. *Hence, when readers were given a literary peek into the Palmers' Lake Shore Drive brownstone, they learned with some amazement that when entertaining at tea in her own parlor, the very correct Mrs. Potter Palmer . . . wore a hat!*

JALAPEÑO CORN BREAD

3 tablespoons corn oil
1 cup cornmeal
2 teaspoons baking powder
1/4 teaspoon baking soda
1 teaspoon salt
1 cup buttermilk

2 eggs, lightly beaten
1 cup cream-style corn
3/4 cup shredded sharp Cheddar
    cheese
1 medium onion, chopped
2 jalapeños, finely chopped

Pour the corn oil into a large cast-iron skillet. Place in a 350-degree oven. Mix the cornmeal, baking powder, baking soda and salt in a large bowl. Add the buttermilk, eggs and corn and mix well. Stir in the cheese, onion and jalapeños. Pour the mixture into the hot skillet. Bake at 350 degrees for 1 hour.

Yield: 6 to 8 servings

Jane Watson

SOUTHERN SPOON BREAD

3/4 cup cornmeal
1 teaspoon salt
3 tablespoons melted butter
1 cup boiling water

1 cup milk
2 eggs, well beaten
2 teaspoons baking powder

Combine the cornmeal, salt and butter in a bowl. Add the boiling water gradually, beating until smooth. Mix in the milk, eggs and baking powder. Pour into a well greased baking dish. Bake at 350 degrees for 45 minutes. Cut into squares and serve with vegetables and meat dishes.

Yield: 8 servings

Cookie Bailey

Zucchini Spoon Bread

1 cup fresh or frozen whole kernel corn
1/2 cup chopped onion
1/2 cup green bell pepper strips
1/2 cup water
1 cup chopped zucchini
1 cup chopped tomatoes

1 cup shredded Cheddar cheese
1/2 cup cornmeal
2 eggs
1/2 cup milk
1/2 teaspoon salt
1/4 teaspoon pepper
Dash of hot pepper sauce

Combine the corn, onion, pepper strips and water in a large saucepan. Bring the mixture to a boil, cover and reduce the heat to a simmer. Simmer for 5 minutes; do not drain. Add the zucchini, tomatoes, cheese and cornmeal. Mix well and set aside. Beat the eggs slightly in a small bowl. Add the milk, salt, pepper and hot pepper sauce. Add the egg mixture to the vegetable mixture and stir until mixed. Pour into a greased 1 1/2-quart casserole. Bake, uncovered, at 350 degrees for 45 to 60 minutes or until set. Let stand for 5 to 10 minutes before serving.

Yield: 6 servings

Lora Hulse

Ham and Egg Breakfast Casserole

12 to 16 very thin bread slices
8 ounces fresh mushrooms, sliced
2 to 4 tablespoons butter
12 ounces shaved ham
2 cups shredded mild Cheddar cheese

6 eggs, beaten
3 cups milk
1/2 teaspoon salt
1/2 teaspoon dry mustard
Bread crumbs

Arrange half the bread slices in a buttered 9x13-inch baking dish. Sauté the mushrooms in butter in a large skillet. Layer the ham, sautéed mushrooms and cheese in the baking dish and cover with a layer of bread slices. Beat the eggs with milk, salt and mustard. Pour the mixture over the layers. Sprinkle the desired amount of crumbs over the top and dot with additional butter. Refrigerate, covered, overnight. Bake at 350 degrees for 1 hour and 20 minutes. Let stand for several minutes before cutting into squares.

Yield: 12 servings

Holli Morris

Train Travel

Many affluent northerners rode down to the Tampa Bay Hotel in private railroad cars, the trains pulling up directly in front of the West Portico. After the guests had strolled into the welcoming lobby and their servants had seen to the piles of luggage, the trains would pull smartly away, depositing the private cars on a spur near the old schoolhouse. When the wondrously sunny resort's Winter Season drew to a close, the private cars would reappear, now brightly cleaned and polished, with a rosebud nodding in each cut-crystal window vase.

Breakfast Pizza

2 (8-count) packages refrigerator
crescent rolls
1 pound bulk sausage
6 eggs, beaten
¹/₂ cup milk

1 cup shredded Cheddar cheese
1 cup shredded mozzarella cheese
Chopped green peppers, mushrooms
or onions (optional)
Oregano and basil to taste

Fit the roll dough into a pizza pan or baking pan. Press the perforations together to seal.
Let the dough rest for several minutes. Bake at 375 degrees for 5 minutes. Cook the sausage in a
large skillet until brown and crumbly, stirring frequently; drain well. Beat the eggs with
the milk. Layer the sausage and cheeses on the partially baked crust. Add the desired amounts of
the optional ingredients and sprinkle with oregano and basil. Pour the egg mixture
over the layers. Bake at 375 degrees for 25 minutes or until the crust is
golden brown and the egg mixture is set.

Yield: 6 servings

Pat Smith

TEXAS EGGS

*This is great for winter brunch, lunch or supper,
especially served with warm curried fruit.*

18 eggs
1/2 cup milk
1/2 cup butter or margarine
1 to 2 cups finely chopped ham
2 (10-ounce) cans cream of mushroom soup

1 (8-ounce) can sliced mushrooms,
  drained
1/2 cup sherry
3/4 cup (or more) shredded sharp
  Cheddar cheese

Beat the eggs with milk in a bowl. Melt the butter in a large skillet. Add the egg mixture
and scramble until soft set. Spoon the eggs into a 9x13-inch baking dish. Combine the ham,
soup, mushrooms and sherry in a saucepan. Cook over medium-low heat until well mixed,
stirring frequently. Pour the mixture over the eggs. Sprinkle with cheese. Refrigerate, covered,
for 1 to 2 days. Bake, uncovered, at 250 degrees for 50 to 60 minutes or until set.
Variation: Cook 1 1/2 to 2 pounds hot sausage in a large skillet until brown and crumbly and
drain well. Substitute for the ham by spreading the sausage in the baking dish and adding the
scrambled eggs. Reduce the soup to just 1 can and replace the sherry with 1/4 soup can of milk.
The mushrooms may be omitted. The dish may be baked immediately, covered, at 350 degrees
for 20 minutes or refrigerated overnight and baked, covered, for 40 minutes.

Yield: 10 to 12 servings

Pat Martin, Lorraine Miller

CHICKEN CREPES

I enjoyed this traditional French birthday breakfast-in-bed in Paris.

4 eggs
1 cup flour
1/2 cup sugar
1 cup (or more) milk

1/4 teaspoon salt
2 tablespoons butter, softened
Chicken Filling

Place the eggs in a blender container and process until frothy. Add the flour, sugar, 1 cup milk and salt and process until smooth. Add additional milk if necessary to make a very thin batter. Butter a 10-inch skillet generously. Heat the skillet over medium-high heat. Add a small amount of the batter to the skillet and tilt the skillet to allow the batter to cover the bottom of the skillet. Cook for 1 to 2 minutes or until the crepe is brown on the bottom. Loosen from the side of the pan, turn the crepe over and cook until brown. Place the crepe on a plate. Spread with a small amount of the Chicken Filling and roll up. Repeat with the remaining batter and filling. Spoon any remaining filling over the crepes.
Variation: Make the crepes for dessert by substituting strawberries, bananas, blueberries, pineapple, peaches or other fruit for the chicken filling.
Top the fruit with sour cream or whipped cream.

CHICKEN FILLING

2 cups chopped cooked
chicken breasts
1 cup sour cream

1 (10-ounce) can cream of
mushroom soup
Nutmeg to taste

Combine the chicken, sour cream, soup and nutmeg in a saucepan. Heat over low heat until well mixed, stirring frequently; do not allow the mixture to boil.

Yield: 12 servings

Cookie Bailey

Infallible Cheese Soufflé

¹/₄ cup butter, softened
10 slices white bread, crusts removed
1¹/₂ cups shredded Cheddar cheese
1¹/₂ cups milk

2 eggs, beaten
¹/₂ teaspoon salt
¹/₄ teaspoon dry mustard
¹/₂ teaspoon paprika
Mushroom Sauce

Butter the bread slices on both sides. Layer the bread slices and shredded cheese ¹/₃ at a time in a 9x13-inch baking dish, ending with the cheese. Beat the milk and eggs in a bowl. Add the salt, dry mustard and paprika and mix well. Pour the egg mixture over the layers. Refrigerate, covered with foil, overnight. Place the dish in a larger pan of hot water. Bake, uncovered, at 350 degrees for 1 hour or until set. Cut into squares and serve with Mushroom Sauce.

Yield: 6 servings

Mushroom Sauce

4 ounces mushrooms, sliced
2 tablespoons butter
2 tablespoons flour

¹/₄ teaspoon salt
¹/₂ cup half-and-half
¹/₂ cup chicken broth

Sauté the mushrooms in 1 tablespoon of the butter and set aside. Melt the remaining butter in a small saucepan. Add the flour and blend well. Add the salt. Stir in the half-and-half and broth gradually. Cook until thickened, stirring constantly. Stir in the sautéed mushrooms and heat to serving temperature.

Yield: 1¹/₂ cups

Barbara Skyrms

BAKED APRICOTS

So good it could be mistaken for dessert.

1 (4-ounce) stack butter crackers
5 (17-ounce) cans apricot halves, drained

²/₃ cup packed light brown sugar
¹/₂ cup melted butter

Roll the crackers into fine crumbs. Alternate layers of the apricots, cracker crumbs and brown sugar in a 3-quart casserole. Drizzle the butter over the top. Bake at 300 degrees for 30 to 45 minutes or until bubbly and top is golden brown.

Yield: 12 servings

Pat Schiff

HOT FRUIT COMPOTE

1 (16-ounce) can sliced peaches
1 (16-ounce) can sliced pears
1 (16-ounce) can pineapple chunks
1 (16-ounce) can pitted sour cherries

1 pound pitted prunes
1 (16-ounce) can applesauce
2 tablespoons sherry
¹/₄ cup crushed macaroons

Drain the canned peaches, pears, pineapple and cherries. Layer the prunes, peaches, pears, pineapple and cherries in a large casserole. Mix the applesauce with the sherry. Spread the applesauce mixture evenly over the layers. Top with the macaroons.
Bake, uncovered, at 300 degrees for 2 hours.

Yield: 10 to 12 servings

Jean Gilbert

CRANBERRY CONSERVE

1 (12-ounce) jar orange
marmalade

1 (12-ounce) jar cranberry sauce
1 cup chopped pecans

Combine the marmalade and cranberry sauce in a bowl and mix well. Stir in the pecans. Spoon into jars or serving bowls. Serve with turkey or chicken as a side dish or on toast for breakfast.

Yield: 4 cups

Cookie Bailey

ANGEL GRITS

4 cups milk
1/2 cup butter
1 cup grits (not instant)
1 teaspoon salt

1/8 teaspoon pepper
1 cup shredded Gruyère cheese
1/3 cup grated Parmesan cheese
1/3 cup melted butter

Scald the milk in a large saucepan; do not boil. Add 1/2 cup butter and cook until the butter melts, stirring constantly. Stir in the grits gradually. Cook for 5 minutes or until the grits are pearl-colored and slightly thickened, stirring constantly. Remove from the heat and pour into a large mixer bowl. Add the salt and pepper and beat until light and fluffy. Pour into a buttered 9x13-inch baking dish. Let stand until cool. Cut the grits into 2-inch squares. Lift the squares and stand the squares on edge, tilting slightly as with dominoes. Sprinkle with the cheeses and drizzle the melted butter over the top. Bake at 400 degrees for 30 to 35 minutes or until brown.

Yield: 10 servings

Ellen McLean

Spinach Cheese Squares

¼ cup butter	1 teaspoon baking powder
3 eggs, beaten	2 (10-ounce) packages frozen
1 cup milk	chopped spinach, thawed
1 cup flour	1 pound Monterey Jack
1 teaspoon salt	cheese, shredded

Melt the butter in a 9x13-inch baking dish in a 350-degree oven. Beat the eggs in a large bowl. Beat in the milk. Mix the flour, salt and baking powder together. Add to the egg mixture and beat until smooth. Drain the spinach well and squeeze out excess moisture. Add the spinach and cheese to the egg mixture and mix well. Pour the mixture into the baking dish. Bake for 35 minutes. Cool for 45 minutes. Cut into bite-size squares. Freeze for future use by arranging the squares on a baking sheet and freezing until firm. Place the frozen squares in sealable plastic bags to store in the freezer. Place the frozen squares on a baking sheet and bake at 325 degrees for 12 minutes before serving.

Yield: 25 squares

Marte Hill

Your Menu, Madame

Dining alone? A lady need feel no trepidation. At the Tampa Bay Hotel a concealed circular staircase led to a screened balcony high above the banqueting hall, where a sequestered table would fully protect a female guest from the embarrassment of unwanted glances. The gallery, later used by an orchestra, imitated those in Moorish architecture which allowed women of the harem to look down, unobserved, upon their lords-and-masters.

TOMATOES ROCKEFELLER

4 firm medium tomatoes	¾ cup melted butter
2 (10-ounce) packages frozen chopped spinach	½ cup grated Parmesan cheese
1 cup soft bread crumbs	½ teaspoon minced garlic
1 cup seasoned bread crumbs	1 teaspoon salt
1 cup finely chopped green onions	1 teaspoon thyme
6 eggs, slightly beaten	Dash of hot pepper sauce
	¼ cup shredded mozzarella cheese

Remove the stems from the tomatoes and cut each tomato into 3 thick slices. Arrange the tomato slices in a single layer in a lightly greased 9x13-inch baking dish. Cook the spinach using the package directions, drain well and squeeze out the excess moisture. Place the spinach in a bowl and add the soft and seasoned bread crumbs, green onions, eggs, melted butter, Parmesan cheese, garlic, salt, thyme and hot pepper sauce and mix well. Spoon the spinach mixture in mounds onto the tomato slices. Sprinkle with the mozzarella cheese. Bake at 350 degrees for 15 minutes or until the spinach mixture is set and the mozzarella cheese is melted.

Yield: 12 servings

Pat Gillen

Yum-Yum Tomatoes

Left-over filling is delicious on baked potatoes.

1 basket cherry tomatoes
8 ounces bacon, crisp-fried, crumbled
1/2 cup mayonnaise
1/3 cup chopped green onions
2 teaspoons minced fresh parsley
3 tablespoons grated Parmesan cheese

Cut the stems from the tomatoes. Scoop out the centers of the tomatoes and invert the tomatoes to drain. Cut a tiny slice from bottoms of the tomatoes to provide a stable base. Combine the bacon, mayonnaise, green onions, parsley and Parmesan cheese in a bowl and mix well. Spoon the bacon mixture into the tomatoes and arrange on a serving platter.

Yield: variable

Taylor Ikin

The "Fair Florida"

Emelia Chapin was a beauty and, having inherited a New York fortune, was also the wealthiest woman around. She and her husband built as their winter residence an incomparably luxurious home on Tampa Bay, with a 61-foot sailboat waiting at the dock. But it was Emelia's private streetcar which made her the envy of Tampa's society matrons. As owner of the streetcar company, Emelia had her "Fair Florida" Pullman done up like a parlor in red plush and wicker. The car, at her beck and call, was connected by spur track to the Chapins' Chateau des Fleurs mansion and Emelia was often seen traveling grandly up and down the Bayshore.

VEGETABLE PIE

*Korean chef Hwang Ki Chong has worked for American
families in Korea since the Korean War. He is my dear and loyal friend who
performed his culinary skills in our home in Korea for more than 5 years.
This is one of KC's memorable recipes.*

1 pound fresh mushrooms, sliced
1 onion, sliced
3 or 4 yellow squash or zucchini,
sliced
1 green bell pepper, sliced
1/4 cup butter
Salt and pepper to taste

Dash of garlic powder
1 cup mayonnaise
3/4 cup grated Parmesan cheese
1 cup shredded mozzarella cheese
1 firm tomato, sliced
1 unbaked (9- or 10-inch) pie shell

Sauté the mushrooms, onion, squash and green pepper in the butter in a large skillet until
tender. Drain well and season with salt, pepper and garlic powder. Combine the mayonnaise,
Parmesan cheese and mozzarella cheese in a bowl and mix well. Arrange the tomato slices in the
pie shell. Add the sautéed vegetables and spread the mayonnaise mixture on top, sealing to the
edge. Bake on the lower oven rack at 350 degrees for 1 hour.

Yield: 6 to 8 servings

Beverly Rogers

Tasty Tomato Pie

This is delicious with our wonderful Ruskin tomatoes, even when made with low-fat mayonnaise and cheese.

1 (10-inch) deep-dish pie shell	¼ teaspoon salt
3 to 4 tomatoes, peeled	¼ teaspoon pepper
6 green onions, chopped (optional)	1 cup mayonnaise
1 tablespoon chopped fresh basil	1 cup shredded Cheddar cheese

Bake the pie shell at 350 degrees until light brown. Slice the tomatoes into thick slices and arrange in the partially baked pie shell. Sprinkle with the green onions, basil, salt and pepper. Mix the mayonnaise with the cheese in a bowl. Spread over the top. Bake for 30 to 40 minutes or until bubbly. Cut into wedges.

Yield: 6 to 8 servings

Jane Hewit, Connie West

Mimosas

2 (12-ounce) cans frozen orange juice concentrate, thawed	1 (16-ounce) jar maraschino cherries
	6 cups extra-dry Champagne, chilled

Dilute 1 can of the orange juice concentrate using the package directions. Pour the juice into ice cube trays. Place 1 cherry in each cube. Freeze the cubes. Dilute the remaining can of orange juice concentrate. Add the Champagne just before serving and mix lightly. Place the ice cubes in glasses. Add the Champagne mixture and garnish with fresh mint sprigs.

Yield: 15 to 20 servings

Nibia Griffin

VEGETABLES

*Plant's steamship races to Cuba
to beat the tobacco embargo.*

CUBA LIBRE!

There were no finer cigars in the world than those
made of the richly aromatic Havana tobaccos.
But 50 years of Spain's debilitating taxation of Cuba was about
to destroy the industry. Reluctantly in 1885 Vicente Ybor and two other
large cigar manufacturers left their homeland and moved workers and equipment
to Tampa, the American port linked to Havana by the Plant Steamship Line.
The area they settled was proudly called Ybor City.
Tampa soon became known as the Cigar Capital of the World, with an annual export
of millions of dollars worth of Havana cigars, loyal Cubans all the while continuing
to transfer guns and money back home. But the Cuban plight worsened.
In 1893, Jose Marti arrived in Ybor City with his stirring cry of "Cuba Libre!"
Cigar-maker patriots pledged a day's pay each week to free Cuba from Spain's oppression
and many smuggled themselves back into Havana desperately to fight the Spanish
garrisons with machetes. Dr. Marti, age 40, was soon killed by the Spaniards
and his cry of "Cuba Libre!" sounded all over America. Infuriated, Spain called for
an embargo on Havana tobacco shipments to the United States. Henry Plant responded
straight away. Racing to reach Havana before the embargo took effect,
Plant loaded tobacco into every inch of his steamers.
Even the luxurious tapestry-lined staterooms of the *Mascotte* and the *Olivette*,
ships named for operas, were packed to their ceilings with the precious leaf.
Because of Plant's bold action, Tampa's cigar industry and the hundreds
of families dependent upon it were saved from certain ruin.
But war was imminent.

Baked Asparagus

2 pounds fresh asparagus spears
¼ teaspoon salt
¼ teaspoon pepper
¼ cup butter
¼ cup chablis

Rinse the asparagus and snap off tough ends. Arrange the asparagus spears in 1 or 2 layers in a baking dish. Season with the salt and pepper and dot with butter. Drizzle the chablis over all. Bake, tightly covered, at 300 degrees for 30 minutes or until the asparagus is tender.

Yield: 8 servings

Pat Gillen

The Acanthus Leaf Design

The acanthus leaf symbolizes admiration of the arts and dates from the days of ancient Greece. It is said that a beautiful young girl of Corinth fell ill and died. Her sorrowing servant placed the girl's trinkets in a basket, covered it with a tile, and nestled it in a small acanthus planted on the grave. By springtime the acanthus had grown vigorously around the basket, its leaves curving gracefully outward upon touching the tile. The charming sight caught the eye of an architect, who copied the plant's shape for a capital. So, to this day, the Corinthian column serves as a remembrance of a lovely child whose life was stilled two and a half thousand years ago.

ASPARAGUS AND TOMATO BUNDLES

4 medium firm ripe tomatoes
1 (15-ounce) can asparagus spears, drained
1/2 cup mayonnaise
2 cups shredded sharp Cheddar cheese

Hot sauce to taste
1/2 teaspoon Worcestershire sauce
3 tablespoons grated onion
6 slices crisp-cooked bacon, crumbled

Cut each tomato into 3 thick slices. Cut the asparagus spears into halves. Layer the tomatoes and asparagus in a buttered shallow baking dish. Combine the mayonnaise, cheese, hot sauce, Worcestershire sauce and onion in a bowl and mix well. Spoon the sauce over the tomatoes and asparagus. Sprinkle the bacon over the top. Bake at 350 degrees for 10 to 15 minutes or until the cheese is melted; do not overbake.

Yield: 6 servings

Pat Gillen

CALICO BEANS

This is a man-pleasing dish at a barbecue.

1 pound bacon	1 (15-ounce) can black-eyed peas
2 pounds lean ground beef	1 (15-ounce) can pinto beans
1½ cups chopped onions	1½ cups catsup
1½ cups chopped celery	2 teaspoons dry mustard
2 (43-ounce) cans baked beans	1½ cups packed brown sugar
1 (15-ounce) can kidney beans	6 tablespoons vinegar

Cook the bacon in a large skillet until crisp; drain, crumble and set aside. Brown the ground beef with the onions and celery in a large skillet, stirring until the ground beef is crumbly and drain well. Place the ground beef mixture in a slow cooker. Add the undrained baked beans, kidney beans, black-eyed peas and pinto beans. Combine the catsup, dry mustard, brown sugar and vinegar in a bowl and mix well. Pour over the beans. Sprinkle the bacon on top. Cook on Low for 6 to 10 hours.

Yield: 12 servings

Charlotte Logan

CARROT SOUFFLÉ

2 cups cooked puréed carrots

2 teaspoons lemon juice

2 tablespoons grated onion

1/2 cup butter, softened

1/4 cup sugar

1 tablespoon flour

1 teaspoon salt

1/4 teaspoon cinnamon

1 cup milk

3 eggs

Combine the carrots, lemon juice, onion, butter, sugar, flour, salt and cinnamon in a mixer bowl and mix well. Add the milk and eggs and beat until smooth and creamy. Pour into a buttered 2-quart casserole. Bake at 350 degrees for 45 to 55 minutes or until the center is firm.

Yield: 8 servings

Pat Gillen

Cauliflower Soufflé

This elegant dish from my husband's mother is marvelous with roast beef.

Florets of 1 head cauliflower
½ cup mayonnaise
3 tablespoons chopped parsley
1 tablespoon lemon juice

1 tablespoon grated onion
Cayenne to taste
3 egg whites

Place the cauliflower in a saucepan with a small amount of water. Cook, covered, over medium heat for 20 minutes or just until tender-crisp. Drain the cauliflower and set aside. Keep the cauliflower hot. Combine the mayonnaise, parsley, lemon juice, onion and cayenne in a bowl and mix well. Beat the egg whites until stiff peaks form. Fold the mayonnaise mixture into the stiffly beaten egg whites. Spoon the cauliflowerets into a baking dish. Spread the egg white mixture over the top. Preheat the broiler. Broil for 3 to 4 minutes or until puffy and light brown.

Yield: 8 to 10 servings

Barbara Starkey

Shipboard

Like all of his ships, the graciously appointed S.S. Evangeline was a compliment to Henry Plant's taste for luxury. Easy chairs, mahogany chests and brass double beds with plump duvets furnished deluxe staterooms. In the dining salon, which seated 150, a small electric lamp glowed on each table. After dinner, the ladies retired to the gold-and-white music room with its rose tapestry, floral carpets and stained glass dome and the gentlemen settled into the oak-and-leather smoke room, where "devotees to My Lady Nicotine" were attentively cared for.

CELERY CASSEROLE

3 cups chopped celery
¼ cup chopped pimento
1 (5-ounce) can sliced water chestnuts,
drained

¼ cup slivered almonds
1 (10-ounce) can cream of chicken soup
¼ cup crushed thin bacon crackers
¾ cup butter, softened

Combine the celery and a small amount of water in a saucepan. Cook over medium heat for 8 minutes or just until tender-crisp; drain. Stir in pimento, water chestnuts, almonds and chicken soup. Spoon into a greased 1½-quart casserole. Sprinkle a mixture of the cracker crumbs and butter over the top. Bake at 350 degrees for 30 to 35 minutes or until bubbly.

Yield: 6 to 8 servings

Lorraine Miller

COLLARD GREENS

An old-time southern recipe from Nancy Fogarty—a genuine southern lady.

1½ pounds lean ham hock
4 quarts water
1 teaspoon lemon pepper
Salt to taste

2 teaspoons sugar
2 teaspoons instant chicken
bouillon
1 bunch collard greens

Cut the ham hock into 1-inch pieces. Bring to a boil with the water in a large saucepan over medium heat. Add the next 4 ingredients. Rinse the collards well. Strip from the center stems and add to the saucepan. Cook over medium heat for 1½ to 2 hours, stirring occasionally.

Yield: 6 to 8 servings

Lorraine Miller

My Favorite Collard Greens

My nurse Bessie used to cook this. Sometimes she would combine collards, mustard greens and turnip greens and we loved that, too—it was so good with corn bread.

3 to 4 pounds collard greens
1 pound salt pork, thick bacon or
ham chunks

2 cups water

Rinse and drain the collard greens 3 or 4 times until all the grit is removed. Strip the leaves from the center stems. Cut the salt pork into cubes. Brown the salt pork in a heavy 4- to 6-quart saucepan over medium heat, stirring frequently. Add the collard greens. Cook until slightly wilted, stirring frequently. Add 2 cups water, or enough to cover. Cook over medium heat for 35 minutes or until the greens are tender, stirring frequently and adding additional water if needed.

Yield: 6 servings

Helen Davis

Corn Pudding

2 (16-ounce) cans white corn	1 cup milk
1/2 cup sugar	1/2 cup melted butter
2 eggs, beaten	1 tablespoon flour

Combine the corn, sugar, eggs and milk in a bowl and mix well. Combine the butter and flour in a small bowl and mix well. Add to the corn and mix well. Spoon into a greased 2-quart baking dish. Bake at 350 degrees for 45 minutes or until thickened and light brown on top.

Yield: 6 servings

Clarajo Hurley

SOCIAL WHIRL

At the start of the Spanish-American War, The Tatler described the brilliant social life at the Tampa Bay Hotel: "The house was launched on a summer season unrivaled since that at a Brussels' hotel preceding the Battle of Waterloo . . . such a gathering of youth and beauty, lovely dark-eyed señoritas in summer gowns, who came in groups to talk to officers 'to learn English,' and the officers chatting with them 'to learn Spanish' . . . There was Richard Harding Davis who was self-conscious to a degree despite the fact that duchesses and others were at his feet . . . . Remington, not unlike the cowboy he describes so well . . . and scores of lesser lights."

Fresh Corn Pudding

This recipe was given to me by Leslie Combs, owner of Spendthrift Farms, Lexington, Kentucky, who got it from his cook who could not remember "when she learned it." For seventeen years, I have looked forward to the Derby and having corn pudding at Leslie's brunch.

4 to 6 ears fresh corn	1 teaspoon salt
6 eggs	1 teaspoon flour
3 cups heavy cream	1/2 teaspoon baking powder
1/2 cup sugar	2 teaspoons melted butter

Cut through just the tips of the corn kernels with a sharp knife and then scrape the cob with the dull edge of the knife to remove the pulp and juice. Measure 3 cups of the corn. Break the eggs into a bowl and stir until well mixed; do not beat. Add the corn and cream and mix well. Mix the sugar, salt, flour and baking powder together. Add to the corn mixture. Stir in the melted butter and mix well. Pour into a greased 9x12-inch baking dish. Bake at 350 degrees for 1 hour or until a knife inserted near the center comes out clean.

Yield: 8 servings

Helen Davis

GREEN BEAN CASSEROLE

*Equally good rewarmed, this can be prepared ahead
of time and refrigerated.*

4 slices bacon
1/2 cup chopped onion
1/2 cup chopped celery
1/4 cup chopped green bell pepper
1 (16-ounce) can tomatoes
1/4 teaspoon salt

1/8 teaspoon pepper
1/2 pound American cheese,
  shredded
2 (16-ounce) cans green beans,
  drained

Microwave the bacon in a microwave-safe dish until crisp. Drain the bacon, reserving
2 tablespoons of the bacon drippings. Drain the bacon on paper towels, crumble and set aside. Add
the onion, celery and green pepper to the reserved bacon drippings in the dish. Microwave on
High for 4 minutes, stirring once or twice. Drain the tomatoes and chop. Add the tomatoes, salt
and pepper to the onion mixture. Microwave on High for 5 minutes. Stir in the cheese. Place the
green beans in a greased 2-quart casserole. Top with the cheese sauce and sprinkle with the
crumbled bacon. Microwave, covered with waxed paper, on Medium for 15 minutes,
rotating the dish once. Garnish with paprika and parsley.

Yield: 4 servings

Sharon Pizzo

Green Tomato Bake

*For those who love fried green tomatoes, this recipe has the same
flavor but none of the drawbacks of frying.*

5 or 6 green tomatoes	¼ teaspoon salt
1 medium onion, chopped	Freshly ground pepper to taste
24 soda crackers, crushed	½ cup buttermilk
1 tablespoon melted butter	

Chop the tomatoes into ¼-inch cubes and place in a large bowl. Add the onion,
cracker crumbs, melted butter, salt and pepper and mix well. Stir in the buttermilk.
Pour into a buttered 2-quart casserole. Bake at 325 degrees for 45 minutes. Brown the
top under a hot broiler for several minutes if desired.

Yield: 6 servings

Betty Wood

LADIES ONLY

*I*nvariably, women guests were enchanted with the double mirror
arrangement. Ever mindful of hiding her ankles and petticoats, a lady
descending the Grand Staircase could pause for an instant on the mirrored
landing and catch her image reflected in the Sitting Room mirror across the
hall. This ladies' parlor was enclosed with the loveliest carved and enameled
woodwork in the hotel, the room having been designed around a mantlepiece
from the Vanderbilt mansion. In the entire history of the hotel no man was
ever known to have stepped into the Sitting Room, though it was
rumored that a woman once entered the Gentlemen's Bar!

HOPPING JOHN

2 cups dried black-eyed peas
2 medium smoked ham hocks
9 cups water
2 medium onions, chopped

1 rib of celery, finely chopped
1 1/2 teaspoons salt
1/2 teaspoon pepper
1 1/2 cups uncooked rice

Sort and rinse the black-eyed peas. Place in a large saucepan with enough water to cover generously. Soak the peas for several hours to overnight. Place the ham hocks in a 5-quart saucepan. Add 8 cups of water or enough to cover the ham hocks. Cover and bring to a boil over medium heat. Reduce the heat to low. Simmer for 1 1/2 hours, stirring occasionally and adding the remaining water if needed. Remove the bones and discard, reserving the ham in the saucepan. Drain the black-eyed peas. Add the peas, onions, celery, salt and pepper to the ham and mix well. Simmer for 45 minutes or until the peas are tender and the liquid is reduced. Stir in the rice. Simmer, covered, for 20 to 30 minutes or until all the liquid is absorbed. Stir with a fork to fluff the mixture.

Yield: 8 servings

Patty Ayala

Mother's Mushroom Business

1 1/2 pounds fresh mushrooms
Butter, softened
12 slices white bread
1 cup chopped onion
1 cup chopped celery
1 cup chopped green bell pepper
1 cup mayonnaise
3/4 teaspoon salt

1/4 teaspoon pepper
2 eggs
1 1/2 cups milk
1 (10-ounce) can cream of mushroom
  soup
2 slices white bread
Shredded sharp Cheddar cheese

Wipe the mushrooms with a damp cloth and cut into thick slices. Sauté the mushrooms in the desired amount of butter in a large skillet. Butter 12 bread slices and cut into 1-inch squares. Combine the mushrooms, onion, celery, green pepper, mayonnaise, salt and pepper in a bowl and mix well. Layer half the bread squares, all the vegetable mixture and the remaining bread squares in a buttered 9x12-inch baking dish. Beat the eggs and milk in a bowl until well mixed and pour over the layers. Chill, covered, for 2 hours to overnight. Spoon the soup over the casserole. Butter the remaining 2 slices of bread and cut into small squares. Sprinkle over the top of the casserole. Bake at 300 degrees for 50 minutes. Sprinkle with cheese. Bake for 10 minutes longer.

Yield: 8 servings

Pat Colvard

ONION PIE

3 medium Vidalia onions,
sliced
3 tablespoons butter
1 partially baked (9-inch)
pie shell
1 cup shredded Swiss cheese

2 egg yolks
2 eggs
1 cup milk
¹/₂ cup whipping cream
1 teaspoon salt
Cayenne to taste

Sauté the onions in the butter in a skillet until limp but not brown. Drain the
sautéed onion and place in the pie shell. Cover with the cheese. Beat the egg yolks
and eggs in a bowl. Add the milk, whipping cream, salt and cayenne and beat until
well blended. Pour over the cheese. Place on the lower oven rack. Bake at
350 degrees for 35 to 40 minutes or until golden brown.

Yield: 8 servings

Sarah Zewadski

CHEESY SCALLOPED POTATOES

4 medium baking potatoes
1/2 medium onion, finely chopped
1 cup evaporated milk
8 to 12 ounces sharp Cheddar cheese, shredded
1/16 teaspoon celery salt

1/16 teaspoon dried chives
1/4 teaspoon parsley
1/2 clove of garlic, minced
Salt and pepper to taste
2 tablespoons margarine or butter

Peel the potatoes and cut into quarters. Cook the potatoes with enough water to cover in a saucepan over medium heat for 20 minutes or until tender. Drain and cool the potatoes and cut into slices. Layer the potatoes in a 1 1/2-quart casserole sprayed with nonstick cooking spray. Add the onion and about half the evaporated milk and sprinkle with half the cheese and all the seasonings. Drizzle with the remaining evaporated milk and sprinkle with the remaining cheese. Dot with the margarine. Bake, covered, at 350 degrees for 40 minutes.

Yield: 4 to 6 servings

Pat Culbreath

DELMONICO POTATOES

10 red potatoes
2 cups half-and-half
2 cups shredded sharp
Cheddar cheese
1¹/₂ teaspoons salt

1 teaspoon dry mustard
Nutmeg and pepper to taste
¹/₄ cup butter
Paprika to taste

Cook the potatoes in water to cover in a saucepan for 25 minutes or until very tender but not mushy. Peel the potatoes and place in a mixer bowl. Beat until the potatoes are mashed. Spoon into a buttered 9x13-inch baking dish. Combine the half-and-half, cheese, salt, mustard, nutmeg and pepper in a saucepan. Heat over medium heat until the cheese melts, stirring constantly. Pour over the potatoes. Chill, covered, for 8 to 10 hours. Dot with butter and sprinkle with paprika. Bake at 325 degrees for 1 hour.

Yield: 12 servings

Ann Thompson

Scallions and Garlic Mashed Potatoes

3 pounds (about 6) medium
baking potatoes
3 scallions
3 cloves of garlic, minced
2 tablespoons butter

1 cup hot milk
6 tablespoons butter, softened
Salt and freshly ground pepper
to taste

Scrub the potatoes and place in a large saucepan with enough water to cover.
Bring to a boil over medium heat. Cook, covered, over low heat for 30 to 40 minutes or until
the potatoes are very tender. Drain, reserving 1 cup of the cooking liquid. Let the
potatoes stand until cool. Cut off and discard all but 1-inch of green on the scallions and mince
the scallions. Sauté the scallions and garlic in 2 tablespoons butter in a skillet until the
scallions are just beginning to brown. Peel the potatoes, cut into chunks and place in a large
mixer bowl. Beat until the potatoes are mashed. Add the 1 cup reserved cooking liquid
and the hot milk. Beat until very smooth. Add the sautéed vegetables, the remaining
6 tablespoons butter and salt and pepper. Beat until light and fluffy. Serve immediately
or place the bowl in a larger container of hot water to keep warm.

Yield: 8 servings

Carole King

CREOLE SPINACH

2 (10-ounce) packages frozen
chopped spinach
8 ounces cream cheese
1/4 cup butter or margarine
Grated rind and juice of 1/2 lemon

Nutmeg, salt and pepper to taste
Cayenne to taste
3/4 cup stuffing mix
1/4 cup melted butter

Cook the spinach using the package directions and drain well. Mix with the cream cheese and 1/4 cup butter in a bowl. Add the lemon rind and juice, nutmeg, salt, pepper and cayenne and mix well. Spoon into a buttered baking dish. Sprinkle the stuffing mix over the top. Drizzle with the melted butter. Bake at 350 degrees for 30 minutes or until brown and bubbly.

Yield: 4 servings

Joan McKay

SPINACH SOUFFLÉ

1 (10-ounce) package frozen spinach,
thawed, drained, squeezed dry
1 cup cottage cheese
3 tablespoons melted margarine

2 eggs, beaten
2 tablespoons flour
1 teaspoon salt
3/4 cup cubed American cheese

Mix the spinach, cottage cheese and margarine in a bowl. Mix the eggs, flour and salt together in a small bowl. Stir into the spinach mixture; add cheese cubes. Spoon into a greased 9-inch square baking dish. Place in a larger pan of hot water. Bake at 350 degrees for 40 minutes or until set.

Yield: 6 servings

Beverly Anderson

Spinach Roulage in Puff Pastry

2 (10-ounce) packages frozen
chopped spinach
1 bunch green onions, sliced
2 tablespoons melted butter
16 ounces dry-curd cottage cheese
1 cup sour cream
1 cup Italian-seasoned bread crumbs

2 tablespoons Pernod
Salt and pepper to taste
2 eggs, beaten
1 (20-ounce) package frozen puff
pastry, thawed
1 tablespoon milk
1 egg

Thaw the spinach, drain well and squeeze dry. Sauté the green onions in the butter
in a skillet. Combine the spinach, sautéed green onions, cottage cheese, sour cream, bread crumbs,
Pernod, salt, pepper and 2 eggs in a bowl and mix well. Place the puff pastry on a flat
surface. Spread the spinach mixture in the center of the pastry. Fold the long edges together to
enclose the spinach mixture and press to seal. Place the spinach roll seam side down on
a buttered baking sheet. Beat the milk with the remaining egg and brush the pastry with the
egg wash. Bake at 400 degrees for 20 to 30 minutes or until puffed and brown.
Let stand for 5 to 10 minutes before slicing.

Yield: 8 servings

Ann Crowder

SPINACH-STUFFED TOMATOES

2 (10-ounce) packages frozen
chopped spinach
1/2 cup chopped onion
1/2 cup butter
1 teaspoon salt
1 cup sour cream
2 teaspoons red wine vinegar

4 fresh tomatoes
Salt and pepper to taste
Melted butter
Grated Parmesan cheese
Bread crumbs
Butter

Cook the spinach using the package directions and drain well. Sauté the onion in
1/2 cup butter in a skillet. Combine the spinach, onion, 1 teaspoon salt, sour cream and vinegar in
a bowl and mix well. Blanch the tomatoes in boiling water and peel. Cut the tomatoes
into halves and scoop out and discard the pulp. Drain the tomato halves. Sprinkle the tomatoes
with salt to taste, pepper, melted butter and Parmesan cheese. Spoon the spinach mixture
into the tomato cups and place on a baking sheet. Sprinkle with Parmesan cheese and bread
crumbs. Dot with butter. Bake at 350 degrees for 15 minutes. The spinach-tomato combination
is especially appropriate for Christmas. The stuffed tomatoes may be prepared the day
before, covered tightly and refrigerated overnight before baking.
Variation: Squash may be substituted for the tomatoes. Cook the squash in salted
water for 10 minutes. Cut into halves and scoop out the seeds. Prepare the spinach
filling as above, fill the squash shells and bake as above.

Yield: 8 servings

Pene Herman

DRIED TOMATOES

16 ripe plum tomatoes or 8 large round tomatoes
1 teaspoon kosher salt
Freshly ground pepper to taste
3 to 4 cloves of garlic, minced
1 bunch fresh basil
2 to 3 teaspoons extra-virgin olive oil

Rinse the tomatoes and pat dry. Cut the plum tomatoes into halves lengthwise or round tomatoes into halves crosswise. Arrange the tomatoes on a baking sheet sprayed with nonstick cooking spray. Sprinkle generously with kosher salt, pepper and garlic. Place 1 basil leaf on each tomato half. Drizzle lightly with the olive oil. Bake at 200 degrees for 12 to 14 hours or until the tomatoes are shrunken, wrinkled and almost dry. Do not allow the tomatoes to dry out completely or they will be tough and do not let them brown. Let the tomatoes stand until cooled to room temperature. Place the dried tomatoes in a sterile jar for storage. May add olive oil to cover if desired and seal the jar with a 2-piece lid. Store in the refrigerator. Tomatoes will keep for 4 to 5 days without the oil and for 6 months with the olive oil.

Yield: about 1 cup

Mary Baker Robbins

Ratatouille Provençale

Good served at room temperature.

1 large eggplant, peeled
Salt
3/4 cup thinly sliced onion
1/3 cup olive oil
2 cloves of garlic, chopped
4 green bell peppers, julienned

3 cups 1/2-inch zucchini slices
2 cups chopped, seeded, peeled
   tomatoes
1/2 cup sliced black olives
1/2 teaspoon oregano
Salt and pepper to taste

Cut the eggplant into slices. Sprinkle with salt and let stand for 30 minutes. Pat dry.
Chop the eggplant and measure 2 1/2 cups for this recipe. Sauté the onion in the olive oil in a
large skillet. Add the garlic and cook for 2 minutes, stirring frequently. Add the
eggplant, green peppers, zucchini, tomatoes, olives and oregano. Simmer, covered,
for 45 minutes over low heat. Simmer, covered, for 15 minutes longer or
until the liquid is reduced, stirring frequently. Add salt and pepper to taste.
Variation: May add yellow squash for color and top with sour cream.

Yield: 8 servings

Kathryn Turner

Squash and Apples

2 pounds butternut squash
5 to 6 tart apples
1/3 cup packed brown sugar
1/4 cup melted butter

1 tablespoon flour
1 teaspoon salt
Ground cloves to taste
1/2 teaspoon mace

Peel the squash and cut into 1/4-inch slices. Peel, core and cut the apples into 1/2-inch wedges. Alternate layers of the squash and apples in a 9x13-inch baking dish sprayed with nonstick cooking spray. Combine the remaining ingredients in a bowl and mix well. Sprinkle over the squash and apples. Bake, covered with foil, at 350 degrees for 1 1/2 hours.

Yield: 12 servings

Pat Schiff

Squash Casserole

2 pounds fresh squash, sliced
1 carrot, grated
1 onion, grated
1 cup sour cream
1/4 cup melted margarine

1 (10-ounce) can cream of
chicken soup
1/2 package herb-seasoned
stuffing mix

Cook the squash in a small amount of water in a saucepan just until tender-crisp and drain well. Combine the squash, carrot, onion, sour cream, margarine and soup in a bowl and mix well. Layer half the stuffing mix, all the squash mixture and the remaining stuffing mix in a greased 9x13-inch baking dish. Bake at 350 degrees for 30 minutes or until brown and bubbly.

Yield: 12 servings

Elaine Watson

BUTTERNUT SQUASH CASSEROLE

1 butternut squash
1 cup sugar
1/2 teaspoon salt
2 eggs, beaten
1/4 cup butter
1/4 cup milk

1 teaspoon vanilla extract
1/2 cup packed brown sugar
1/3 cup flour
1/4 cup butter
1/2 cup chopped pecans

Cut the squash into halves lengthwise and scoop out and discard the seeds. Place the squash in a shallow baking dish with 1/2 inch water. Bake at 350 degrees for 1 hour or until the squash is tender. Drain the squash well and scoop out and mash enough squash pulp to measure 3 cups. Combine the squash, sugar, salt, eggs, 1/4 cup butter, milk and vanilla in a bowl and mix well. Spoon into a buttered baking dish. Combine the brown sugar, flour, remaining 1/4 cup butter and pecans in a bowl and mix well. Sprinkle over the squash mixture. Bake at 350 degrees for 45 minutes or until brown and bubbly.

Yield: 6 servings

Charla Wash

Retreat Squash Casserole

A friend who lived on the 18th century estate "Retreat" in Essex County, Virginia, shared this recipe.

2 pounds yellow squash
2 (10-ounce) cans cream of celery soup
2 medium onions, chopped
2 cups sour cream
1 (2-ounce) jar chopped pimento

1 (8-ounce) can sliced water chestnuts, drained
Salt and pepper to taste
1 (8-ounce) package seasoned stuffing mix
1/4 cup melted butter

Coarsely chop the squash. Cook the squash in a small amount of salted water in a saucepan just until tender-crisp and drain well. Combine the soup, onions, sour cream, pimento, water chestnuts, salt and pepper in a bowl and mix well. Layer half the stuffing mix, all the squash, all the soup mixture and the remaining stuffing mix in a large buttered baking dish. Bake at 350 degrees for 30 to 45 minutes or until brown and bubbly.

Yield: 12 to 15 servings

Nell Lee Keen

Senator Russell's Sweet Potatoes

3 cups mashed cooked
sweet potatoes
2 eggs
1 cup sugar
1 teaspoon vanilla extract
1/2 cup melted butter or margarine

1 cup packed brown sugar
1/3 cup flour
1 cup chopped nuts
1/3 cup butter or margarine,
softened

Combine the sweet potatoes, eggs, sugar, vanilla and melted butter in a bowl and mix well.
Spoon into a greased baking dish. Combine the brown sugar, flour, nuts and remaining butter in a
bowl and mix well. Sprinkle over the sweet potatoes. Bake at 350 degrees for 30 minutes.

Yield: 6 servings

Nancy Segall

Rum and Coca-Cola

*During the Spanish-American War, the officers awaiting assignment to
battle marked time in Tampa at Henry Plant's hotel. The waiting had its
compensations. Not only was the hotel the last word in luxury, but the
Gentlemen's Bar could pour anything from Cuban rum to the new soft
drink from Atlanta called Coca-Cola. A combination of the two beverages was
served up with the toast "Cuba Libre!" and a popular highball was born.*

CAKES, COOKIES & PIES

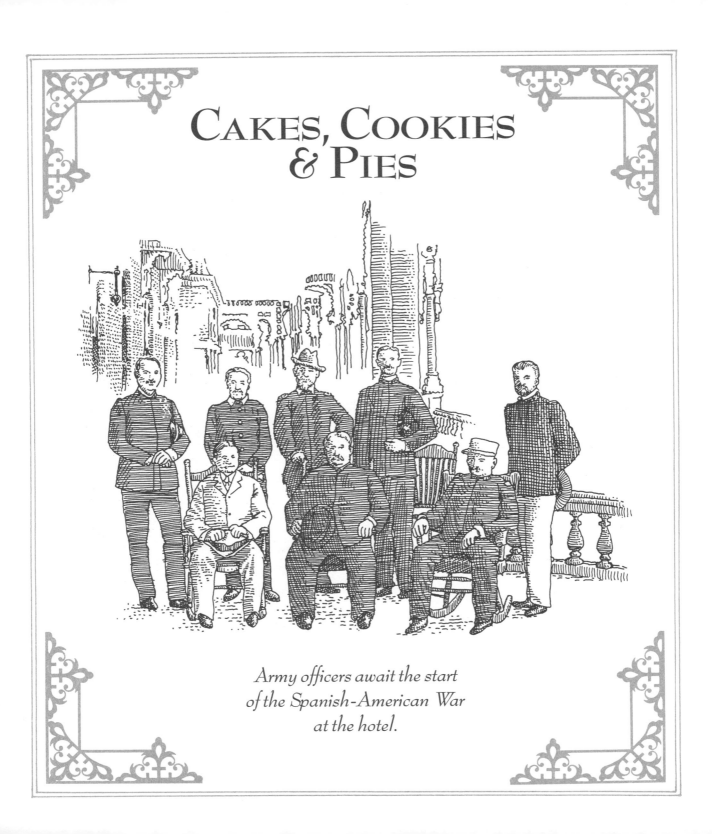

*Army officers await the start
of the Spanish-American War
at the hotel.*

THE ROCKING
CHAIR WAR

It was on February 15, 1898, that Spain blew up the battleship *Maine*
in Havana Harbor. Survivors and refugees by the hundreds arrived in Tampa on H.B.
Plant ships, shouting, "Remember the *Maine*! Down with Spain!" In answer to demands
for Cuban independence, Spain declared war. Thirty thousand soldiers were rushed to Tampa
by the only means possible—on Plant railroad lines—but two thousand of them died
of yellow fever before seeing action. The Army commander accepted Plant's offer
to use the Tampa Bay Hotel as Headquarters, but the aging general, who believed in sharing
his troops' miseries, spent his nights rolled in a blanket out on the veranda's wood floor.
For weeks officers lounged in hotel rocking chairs awaiting the start of hostilities,
giving rise to the sobriquet for the Spanish-American War. Plant was an elderly man
of 79 at this time, but continued to make decisions as he had done all his adult life.
Directing operations at Port Tampa, he was confronted by a young Army officer
who had the temerity to suggest that, should Plant not stick to minding his own business
at the hotel, the War Department might very well step in and take over his entire enterprise.
Never one to mince words, Plant retorted, "Seize it and be damned!" and turned his back—
on Teddy Roosevelt. Teddy, his Rough Riders and the 10th Cavalry soon set sail for Cuba.
After two months and San Juan Hill it was all over. Plant converted his steamers
into hospital ships and brought the wounded back home to Tampa.

APPLESAUCE CAKE

2¹/₂ cups hot applesauce	2 teaspoons cinnamon
1 cup shortening	1 cup chopped nuts
2 cups sugar	1 pound white raisins
3 cups flour	1 pound currants
1 teaspoon salt	4 ounces citron
2 teaspoons cloves	1 cup flour
1 teaspoon allspice	2 teaspoons baking soda

Pour 2 cups of the hot applesauce into a large bowl. Set the remaining ¹/₂ cup applesauce aside. Add the shortening and sugar to the hot applesauce and stir until the shortening melts. Sift 3 cups flour with the salt and spices. Add to the applesauce mixture and mix well. Combine the nuts, raisins, currants and citron in a bowl. Sprinkle the remaining cup flour over the mixture and mix until coated. Add to the applesauce mixture and mix well. Stir the baking soda into the reserved hot applesauce. Add to the batter and mix well. Pour into a greased and floured 4-inch-deep baking pan. Bake at 300 degrees for 1 hour or until the cake tests done.

Yield: 16 to 20 servings

Mary Baker Robbins

SPANISH KEYHOLE ARCH DESIGN

Many Victorian architects were aghast at their new industrialized world and turned to the past or to the foreign for inspiration, resurrecting the spiritual in Gothic trefoils and calling up sensual associations with Spanish keyhole arches and Near Eastern minarets. This exotica draped a film of fantasy over the truth of Victorian life.

CHOCOLATE ALMOND TORTE

You can make your own almond meal for this recipe by processing unsalted blanched almonds in a blender or food processor.

8 ounces semisweet chocolate, broken
2¹/₂ tablespoons milk
³/₄ cup ground blanched almond meal
¹/₂ cup sugar
6 egg yolks, beaten

1 teaspoon vanilla extract
1 teaspoon almond extract (optional)
6 egg whites
1 recipe 7-minute frosting
Shredded coconut to taste

Combine the chocolate and milk in a double boiler over hot water. Heat until the chocolate is melted and well blended. Combine the melted chocolate, almond meal, sugar, egg yolks and the vanilla and almond extracts in a large bowl and beat until well mixed. Beat the egg whites in a mixer bowl until stiff peaks form. Fold the stiffly beaten egg whites gently into the chocolate batter. Pour into a greased and floured springform pan or a round 1¹/₂x9-inch cake pan. Bake at 375 degrees for 40 to 45 minutes or until a cake tester inserted in the center comes out clean. Cool the torte in the pan on a wire rack. Loosen the torte from the side of the pan and turn onto a wire rack. Frost with your favorite recipe for 7-minute frosting and sprinkle with coconut. The crust may be softened by wrapping tightly and storing overnight before frosting.

Yield: 8 servings

Marjorie Christopher

MAURICIO'S SPANISH BRANDY CAKE

*A Mexican mother's treasured recipe—blessedly shared with her son, Mauricio,
who now enjoys making it for special occasions.*

1 cup butter, softened	4 cups sifted flour
1¼ cups sugar	1 tablespoon baking powder
4 jumbo eggs	⅛ teaspoon salt
3 ounces good Spanish brandy	½ cup (about) milk
(such as El Presidente)	Almonds

Cream the butter and sugar in a bowl until light and fluffy. Add the eggs and beat at low
speed until well blended. Beat in the brandy gradually. Mix the flour with the baking powder and
salt. Add to the batter gradually, beating constantly at low speed until well mixed. Add just
enough milk to make the mixture of pourable consistency. Pour the batter into a buttered
tube pan with a removable bottom. Sprinkle with almonds. Bake at 400 degrees for 45 minutes
or until a wooden pick inserted in the center comes out clean. The top will be cracked,
brown and beautiful. Cool in the pan on a wire rack. Loosen the cake
from the side of the pan and turn onto a cake plate.

Yield: 12 to 16 servings

Sarah Jane Rubio

ClaraJane's Fudge Cake

*A tradition at The Chiseler's Market Snack Bar, Red Cross Angels
Coffee, Easter Seal Guild Coffee, Cross of Lorraine Coffee,
Hearts of Gold Coffee and many other occasions.*

2 (1-ounce) squares unsweetened chocolate	³/₄ cup flour, sifted
¹/₂ cup butter	1 cup broken pecans
1 cup sugar	1 to 2 tablespoons flour
2 eggs, beaten	1 to 2 cups miniature marshmallows
	Fudge Frosting

Melt the chocolate and butter in a double boiler over hot water or in a small microwave-safe bowl in the microwave and stir until well blended. Combine the sugar and eggs in a large bowl and beat until well mixed. Add the chocolate mixture and blend well. Add the sifted flour and mix well. Sprinkle the pecans with just enough flour to coat lightly. Stir into the cake batter. Pour the batter into a greased and waxed-paper-lined 9-inch-square baking pan. Bake at 325 degrees for 15 to 20 minutes or until set. Invert the hot cake onto waxed paper. Cover with miniature marshmallows. Pour the hot Fudge Frosting over the hot cake and spread to cover the cake. Let stand until the cake and frosting are cool and firm. Cut into squares.

Fudge Frosting

2 cups confectioners' sugar	¹/₄ cup butter
¹/₂ cup baking cocoa	¹/₄ cup milk
¹/₈ teaspoon salt	

Sift the confectioners' sugar, cocoa and salt into a bowl. Combine the butter and milk in a small saucepan and heat until the butter melts. Add to the cocoa mixture and mix well.

Yield: 8 to 12 servings

Beverly Austin

Cakes, Cookies & Pies

Chocolate Pound Cakes

3$^{1}/_{3}$ cups flour	3 cups sugar
$^{1}/_{2}$ cup baking cocoa	5 eggs
$^{1}/_{4}$ teaspoon salt	1 cup sour cream
1 teaspoon baking powder	1 cup boiling water
1$^{1}/_{2}$ cups butter, softened	2 teaspoons vanilla extract

Mix the flour, cocoa, salt and baking powder in a bowl. Cream the butter in a large bowl. Add the sugar gradually, beating constantly. Beat for 5 to 7 minutes. Beat in the eggs 1 at a time. Add the flour mixture to the creamed mixture alternately with the sour cream, beginning and ending with the flour mixture and mixing just until the batter is smooth; do not overmix. Add the boiling water and vanilla and mix well. Pour the batter into 2 greased and floured 5x9-inch loaf pans. Bake at 325 degrees for 60 to 75 minutes or until a cake tester inserted in the center comes out clean. Cool in the pans on a wire rack for 10 minutes. Remove from the pans to wire racks to cool completely. Wrap the loaves tightly and store in the refrigerator or freezer. Margarine may be substituted for the butter.

Yield: 2 loaves

Anita Gillen

Boys Will Be Boys

Tampa will never forget the Rough Riders, although their colorful sojourn lasted only a week before they headed off to war. The elite hand-picked regiment roared into Tampa "with excessive glee," shooting up the local theater house and then driving their horses through the front doors of a popular eating place. The bewildered restaurateur responded to this swagger by buying drinks all around and a group of nuns prayed for the troops' salvation and fed them home-cooked meals.

Coconut Pound Cake

This cake is great for dessert, tea, breakfast, or box lunches.

1 (2-layer) package yellow cake mix
¹/₂ cup sugar
²/₃ cup vegetable oil
4 eggs

1 cup sour cream
1 (12-ounce) package frozen coconut
Coconut Glaze

Combine the cake mix, sugar, oil, eggs and sour cream in a large mixer bowl. Beat the mixture at medium to high speed for 3 to 4 minutes or until well blended. Fold in the coconut. Pour into a greased and floured large bundt pan. Bake at 325 degrees for 1 hour or until the cake tests done. Invert the hot cake onto a cake plate. Drizzle the Coconut Glaze over the warm cake.

Coconut Glaze

1 cup confectioners' sugar
2 tablespoons milk

¹/₄ teaspoon coconut extract or
vanilla extract

Combine the confectioners' sugar, milk and coconut extract in a small bowl and blend until smooth.

Yield: 12 to 16 servings

Patsy McNichols

LOVELY COCONUT CAKE

1 cup butter, softened	1/8 teaspoon salt
2 cups sugar	1 cup buttermilk
5 eggs	1 teaspoon vanilla extract
2 3/4 cups cake flour	3/4 teaspoon coconut extract
1 teaspoon baking powder	2 recipes Never-Fail Frosting
1 teaspoon baking soda	2 cups frozen grated coconut

Cream the butter and sugar in a large bowl with an electric mixer for 10 minutes or until very light and fluffy. Beat in the eggs 1 at a time. Sift the flour, baking powder, baking soda and salt together. Add to the creamed mixture alternately with the buttermilk, beating well after each addition. Stir in the vanilla and coconut extracts. Pour the batter into 3 greased and floured 9-inch cake pans. Bake at 350 degrees for 25 minutes or until the layers test done. Cool in the pans on wire racks for 10 to 15 minutes. Remove to the wire racks to cool completely. Spread the Never-Fail Frosting and sprinkle with coconut between the layers and over the top of the cake.

NEVER-FAIL FROSTING

Make two batches of the frosting; do not attempt to double the recipe.

1 cup sugar	2 egg whites
1/4 teaspoon salt	3 tablespoons water
1/2 teaspoon cream of tartar	1 teaspoon vanilla extract

Combine the sugar, salt, cream of tartar, egg whites and water in the top of a double boiler over boiling water. Beat with an electric mixer at high speed for about 3 minutes or until the frosting is fluffy and holds its shape. Remove from the heat and beat in the vanilla.

Yield: 16 servings

Carol Mathews

COMPANY GRAHAM CRACKER CAKE

*My husband's grandmother gave me this recipe when we were first married. It
was my specialty as a young bride and used only for "company."*

1/2 cup margarine, softened

1 cup sugar

2 egg yolks, beaten

1 3/4 cups graham cracker crumbs

1 1/2 teaspoons baking powder

1 cup milk

1/2 cup chopped pecans

2 egg whites

1 cup crushed pineapple

1 cup sugar

Cream the margarine and 1 cup sugar in a large bowl until light and fluffy. Add the egg
yolks and beat until blended. Mix the graham cracker crumbs and baking powder together. Add
to the creamed mixture alternately with milk, mixing well after each addition. Add the
pecans and mix well. Beat the egg whites until stiff peaks form. Fold the stiffly beaten egg whites
gently into the pecan mixture. Spread the batter evenly in a greased 9x13-inch cake pan.
Bake at 350 degrees for 35 minutes. Cool the cake in the pan on a wire rack. Combine the
undrained pineapple and 1 cup sugar in a saucepan. Bring to a boil and boil for
5 minutes, stirring constantly. Spoon the pineapple mixture over the cooled cake.
Cut into squares and serve with a dollop of whipped cream.

Yield: 8 to 10 servings

Marte Hill

MINCEMEAT CAKE

Hard Sauce Rum Balls are a must with this!

1 (2-layer) package applesauce cake mix
3 eggs
1/4 cup water
3 cups mincemeat
1 cup chopped nuts
Light corn syrup

Beat all ingredients except corn syrup in a mixer bowl at medium speed for 2 minutes. Pour into a greased and floured 10-inch tube pan. Bake at 350 degrees for 50 to 60 minutes or until the cake tests done. Cool in the pan for 15 minutes. Invert onto a wire rack to cool completely. Brush the cake on all sides with corn syrup. Pour brandy over the cake and ignite if desired.

Yield: 10 to 12 servings

Susie Sanders

HARD SAUCE RUM BALLS

1 cup butter or margarine, softened
1 (13-ounce) package vanilla frosting mix
2 eggs
1 tablespoon rum or rum extract

Combine the butter and frosting mix in a large bowl and beat until well mixed. Add the eggs and rum and beat until fluffy. Refrigerate, covered, until firm. Use a melon baller to scoop the mixture into balls. Refrigerate, covered. Serve with Mincemeat Cake or English puddings.

Yield: 10 to 12 servings

Susie Sanders

ORANGE NUT CAKE

1 cup margarine, softened	4 eggs
2 cups sugar	2 tablespoons grated orange rind
3 cups flour	1 cup chopped pecans
1/2 teaspoon salt	1 cup chopped dates
1 teaspoon baking soda	1 cup shredded coconut
1/2 cup buttermilk	Orange Glaze

Cream the margarine and 2 cups sugar in a large bowl until light and fluffy. Mix the flour and salt together. Reserve a small amount of the flour mixture. Dissolve the baking soda in the buttermilk. Add the eggs to the creamed mixture and beat until well blended. Add the remaining flour mixture and the buttermilk mixture to the creamed mixture alternately, beating well after each addition. Stir in the orange rind. Combine the pecans and dates in a bowl. Add the reserved flour and mix until coated. Add to the batter and mix well. Mix in the coconut. Pour into a greased and floured tube pan. Bake at 325 degrees for 1 1/2 hours or until the cake tests done. Prick holes in the cake. Pour the hot Orange Glaze over the cake very slowly to allow the cake to absorb the mixture. Let the cake stand until cool. Invert onto a cake plate.

ORANGE GLAZE

1 cup orange juice	1 1/2 cups sugar

Combine the orange juice and sugar in a saucepan. Bring to a boil, stirring until the sugar dissolves completely.

Yield: 12 to 16 servings

Alice Dingle

Bess Ferman's Pound Cake

A Jimmy Ferman specialty!

1¹/₂ cups butter, softened   2¹/₃ cups sugar
3 cups cake flour   2 teaspoons baking powder
¹/₂ teaspoon salt   2 teaspoons vanilla extract
8 eggs

Cream the butter in a large mixer bowl. Add the flour and salt and beat until light. Beat the eggs in a small mixer bowl at high speed for 2 to 3 minutes. Mix the sugar with the baking powder and add to the eggs gradually, beating constantly. Beat for 2 to 3 minutes. Add the sugar mixture to the flour mixture gradually, beating constantly. Beat in the vanilla. Beat at low speed for 2 minutes. Spoon into a lightly greased tube pan or 2 paper-lined loaf pans. Bake at 310 degrees for 60 to 70 minutes for the tube pan or 55 to 60 minutes for the loaf pans or until the cake tests done. Loosen the cake from the tube pan. Let stand until cool. Invert the cake onto a cake plate.

Yield: 1 large cake or 2 loaves

Martha Ferman, Charter Member

Car Number 100

Brass lamps with milk-glass shades hung from the mahogany ceiling, the table was covered with a paisley shawl and swags of heavy velvet draped the many windows in Henry Plant's Victorian office. There was no finer private car on any railroad line, Car Number 100. Henry worked in it, ate in it and slept in it for many years, shuttling back and forth along the Plant Lines, always managing to be at the right place at the right time to handle any problem developing in his transportation system of railroads, steamships and hotels.

THREE-FLAVOR POUND CAKE

This is the first recipe that I asked for in Tampa—from Jenny Turner. I have served it with elegant ice creams, as well as for school dinners and picnics. It freezes beautifully and makes the best breakfast toast or coffee cake.

1 cup butter, softened
2 cups sugar
6 eggs
2 cups flour
1/2 teaspoon baking powder

1/8 teaspoon salt
1/8 teaspoon mace or nutmeg
1 teaspoon vanilla extract
1 teaspoon almond extract

Cream the butter and sugar in a mixer bowl until light and fluffy. Add the eggs 1 at a time, beating well after each addition. Mix the flour, baking powder, salt and mace together. Add to the creamed mixture gradually, beating constantly until well blended. Add the vanilla and almond extracts and beat well. Pour into a greased and floured tube pan. Bake at 300 degrees for 60 to 70 minutes or until the cake tests done. Cool in the pan on a wire rack. Invert onto a cake plate.

Yield: 12 servings

Susie Sanders

Pumpkin Roll

3 eggs
2/3 cup pumpkin purée
1 cup sugar
3/4 cup flour
1 teaspoon baking powder

1/2 teaspoon cinnamon
1 cup chopped pecans
Sugar
Cream Cheese Filling

Line a 10x15-inch cake pan with waxed paper. Combine the eggs, pumpkin and 1 cup sugar in a large bowl and beat until well blended. Mix the flour, baking powder and cinnamon together. Add to the pumpkin mixture and beat until blended. Stir in the pecans. Pour into the prepared pan, spreading the batter evenly. Bake at 375 degrees for 15 minutes. Invert the cake onto a tea towel covered with additional sugar. Roll the cake in the tea towel as for a jelly roll. Let stand until completely cooled. Unroll the cake and remove the towel. Spread the cake with the Cream Cheese Filling and reroll. Chill until serving time.

Cream Cheese Filling

2 tablespoons butter or margarine, softened
8 ounces cream cheese, softened

3/4 teaspoon vanilla extract
1 cup confectioners' sugar

Combine the butter and cream cheese in a small bowl and beat until smooth and creamy. Beat in the vanilla. Add the confectioners' sugar gradually, beating constantly until light and fluffy.

Yield: 6 to 8 servings

Carole King

ANGEL IN THE CLOUDS

1 package angel food cake mix
1 1/2 cups Nestlé Quik chocolate
drink mix powder

3 cups whipping cream
1 1/2 cups confectioners' sugar
1 1/2 teaspoons vanilla extract

Prepare the cake mix using the package directions. Cool and remove from the cake pan. Cut the cake into 3 horizontal layers. Mix the chocolate drink mix and whipping cream in a large mixer bowl. Beat in the confectioners' sugar and vanilla until stiff peaks form; do not overbeat. Place the bottom layer on a cake plate. Spread the whipped cream mixture between the cake layers and over the top and side of the cake. Cover the cake. Refrigerate for 8 hours to overnight.

Yield: 10 servings

Sallie Holmberg

PECAN BUTTERSCOTCH BARS

1/2 cup butter
1 cup packed brown sugar
1 egg
1 teaspoon vanilla extract

1 cup sifted flour
1 teaspoon baking powder
1/8 teaspoon salt
1/2 to 1 cup chopped pecans

Melt the butter. Combine the melted butter and the brown sugar in a bowl and mix until blended. Let stand until cool. Add the egg and vanilla; beat until well mixed. Sift the flour, baking powder and salt together. Add to the brown sugar mixture and mix well. Stir in the pecans. Spread the mixture evenly in an 8-inch square baking pan. Bake at 300 degrees for 40 minutes or until golden brown. Let stand until cool. Cut into bars.

Yield: 16 bars

Laura Bentley

DOUBLE-FUDGE BROWNIES

2 (1-ounce) squares unsweetened chocolate
1/2 cup butter
2 eggs
1 cup sugar
1/2 cup sifted flour
1/4 teaspoon salt
1 teaspoon vanilla extract
1/2 cup chopped nuts
Fudge Frosting
3 (1-ounce) squares unsweetened or semisweet chocolate

Melt 2 squares of the chocolate and butter and blend well. Beat the eggs in a bowl. Add the sugar and beat until well blended. Add the chocolate mixture and blend well. Sift the flour and salt together and add to the chocolate mixture. Add the vanilla and mix well. Stir in the nuts. Spread the mixture evenly in a greased 7x11-inch baking pan. Bake at 350 degrees for 20 to 25 minutes or until the brownies pull from the sides of the pan. Cool in the pan on a wire rack. Spread the Fudge Frosting over the top. Melt the remaining 3 ounces chocolate and spread over the frosting. Chill in the refrigerator. Cut into small squares and place the squares in small bonbon cups for a special serving presentation. Store the brownies in the refrigerator but bring to room temperature before serving.

FUDGE FROSTING

1 1/2 cups sugar
1/3 cup butter
1/2 cup medium cream
1 teaspoon vanilla extract

Combine the sugar, butter and cream in a saucepan. Cook over low heat until the butter melts and the sugar is dissolved, stirring constantly. Cook the mixture to 236 degrees on a candy thermometer, soft-ball stage. Place the saucepan in a larger pan of cold water. Let stand until cool. Add the vanilla and beat until creamy.

Yield: variable

Diane Kemker

Gooey Turtle Bars

This is such an easy recipe, and the cookies can be frozen, too. I crush the vanilla wafers and chop the pecans in the food processor.

1½ cups vanilla wafer crumbs
½ cup melted butter
2 cups semisweet chocolate chips

1 cup chopped pecans
1 cup caramel topping

Combine the crumbs and butter in a bowl and mix well. Press evenly over the bottom of a 9x13-inch baking pan. Sprinkle with the chocolate chips and pecans. Microwave the caramel topping on High for 1½ minutes, stirring every 30 seconds. Drizzle over the chocolate chips and pecans. Bake at 350 degrees for 12 to 15 minutes or until the chocolate chips melt. Cool in the pan on a wire rack for 30 minutes or longer before cutting into bars.

Yield: 4 dozen

Pat Gillen

MAN'S BEST FRIEND

Some thought him lucky, but northern hunters praised Arthur Schleman as one of the country's top hunting guides. When the Tampa Bay Hotel closed its doors, Schleman gave up tracking bear and panther to serve as city dog catcher, a position of not inconsiderable importance because of the large number of rabid dogs in the South. One snarly creature even bit Schleman on the leg—his wooden leg, as luck would have it.

Confetti Cookies

1 cup sugar	2 1/2 cups flour
1/2 cup packed brown sugar	1 teaspoon salt
1 cup shortening	1 teaspoon baking soda
2 eggs	1 cup chopped gumdrops
1 teaspoon vanilla extract	1 cup chopped nuts

Cream the sugar, brown sugar and shortening in a large bowl until light and fluffy.
Add the eggs and vanilla and beat until blended. Mix the flour, salt and baking soda together. Add
to the creamed mixture and mix well. Sprinkle the gumdrops with a small amount of
additional sugar and mix until coated to facilitate mixing the gumdrops into the cookie dough.
Stir in the gumdrops and nuts. Drop by teaspoonfuls onto a greased cookie sheet.
Bake at 350 degrees for 8 to 10 minutes or until golden brown. Cool on the cookie sheet
for 1 to 2 minutes and remove to a wire rack to cool completely.

Yield: 5 dozen

Cookie Bailey

CARMELITAS

1 (16-ounce) roll refrigerated chocolate
chip cookie dough
1 cup semisweet chocolate chips

32 vanilla caramels
¼ cup light cream
½ cup (or more) chopped pecans

Slice the cookie dough about ¼ inch thick and arrange in a 9-inch square baking pan. Bake at 375 degrees for 25 minutes or until lightly browned. Sprinkle the chocolate chips over the warm baked cookie dough. Combine the caramels and cream in a saucepan. Heat over low heat until the caramels are melted and well blended with the cream. Spread the caramel mixture over the top and sprinkle with the pecans. Let stand until cool before cutting into squares.

Yield: 2 to 3 dozen

Betty Farrior

TOFFEE SQUARES

1 cup butter, softened
1 cup packed brown sugar
1 egg yolk
1 teaspoon vanilla extract

2 cups flour
1 cup chocolate chips
½ cup chopped nuts

Combine the butter and brown sugar in a bowl and mix until well blended. Add the egg yolk and vanilla and mix well. Add the flour and mix well. Pat evenly into a 10x15-inch baking pan. Bake at 350 degrees for 20 minutes or until light brown. Sprinkle the chocolate chips over the top. Let stand for about 2 minutes to soften, then spread the melted chocolate. Sprinkle with nuts. Cut into squares while warm.

Yield: 3 to 4 dozen

Elaine Newman

KEY LIME COOKIES

1 cup flour	5 tablespoons Key lime juice
1/4 cup confectioners' sugar	1 cup sugar
1/2 cup butter, softened	2 tablespoons flour
2 eggs	

Mix the 1 cup flour and confectioners' sugar in a bowl. Add the butter and mix
until crumbly. Press into a 9x9-inch baking pan. Bake at 350 degrees for 10 minutes. Remove
from the oven. Beat the eggs in a small bowl. Add the Key lime juice and beat
until blended. Mix the sugar with 2 tablespoons flour. Add to the egg mixture and beat until
smooth. Pour over the baked layer. Bake at 350 degrees for 20 minutes.
Cool in the pan on a wire rack. Cut into squares.

Yield: 3 dozen

Martha Hall

OATMEAL COOKIES

3 eggs, well beaten	2½ cups flour
1 teaspoon vanilla extract	2 teaspoons baking soda
1 cup raisins	1 teaspoon salt
1 cup sugar	1 teaspoon ground cinnamon
1 cup packed brown sugar	2 cups rolled oats
1 cup butter, softened	¾ cup chopped nuts

Beat the eggs with the vanilla in a medium bowl. Add the raisins and mix well.
Let stand, covered with plastic wrap, for 1 hour. Cream the sugar, brown sugar and butter in a
large bowl until light and fluffy. Mix the flour, baking soda, salt and cinnamon
together. Add to the creamed mixture and mix well. Add the raisin mixture, oats and nuts and
mix well; the dough will be stiff. Drop by heaping teaspoons onto an ungreased cookie
sheet or shape the dough into small balls, arrange on the cookie sheet and flatten slightly.
Bake at 350 degrees for 10 to 12 minutes or until light brown. Cool on the cookie sheet
for 1 to 2 minutes. Remove to a wire rack to cool completely.

Yield: 6 dozen

Mary Baker Robbins

MAURICIO'S PASTELITOS
MILITARES DE PARIS

These little pastries are known to the Rubio family as the "little military men of Paris" even though they bear no resemblance.

2½ cups flour
7 tablespoons sugar
1 cup butter, softened
4 egg yolks

Grated rind of 2 lemons
1 tablespoon vanilla extract
Sugar
Orange marmalade

Combine the flour and 7 tablespoons sugar in a large mixer bowl. Add the butter and mix with an electric mixer fitted with dough hooks at low speed. Add the egg yolks, lemon rind and vanilla and continue to beat until the mixture forms a ball. Shape the dough into 1½-inch-diameter balls, roll in sugar to coat well and arrange on a greased cookie sheet. Make a thumb-size depression in the center of each. Fill with marmalade. Bake at 400 degrees for 15 minutes or until light golden brown. Watch carefully as they burn easily. Cool on the cookie sheet for 1 to 2 minutes. Remove to a wire rack to cool completely.

Yield: 2 dozen

Sarah Jane Rubio

FRUITED CHESS PIE

½ cup melted butter	½ cup golden raisins
1 cup sugar	½ cup chopped pecans
2 eggs, beaten	1 tablespoon vinegar
½ cup shredded coconut	1 unbaked (9-inch) pie shell

Combine the butter and sugar in a bowl and blend well. Add the eggs and mix until smooth. Stir in the coconut, raisins and pecans. Add the vinegar and mix well. Pour into the pie shell. Bake at 325 degrees for 40 minutes or until the center is set and the crust is golden brown. Cool on a wire rack.

Yield: 8 servings

Judy Rodriguez

ALL OPPOSED, NAY

Henry Plant spent $2.5 million constructing his most remarkable hotel and $500,000 decorating it with antiques from around the world. In 1905, six years after Plant died, his heirs sold to the city the magnificent structure, its furnishings and the acres of prime real estate on which it sat, for $125,000. One of the city councilmen voted against it, complaining the price was too high.

PEACHES AND CREAM PIE

8 fresh peaches
Salt to taste
Lemon juice to taste
1 unbaked (9-inch) pie shell

Topping
2 tablespoons butter
2 teaspoons cinnamon

Peel and slice the peaches and place in a large bowl. Sprinkle with salt and lemon juice and mix gently. Arrange the peach slices in the pie shell. Pour the Topping over the peaches. Dot with butter and sprinkle with cinnamon. Bake at 425 degrees for 15 minutes. Reduce the temperature to 300 degrees. Bake for 40 to 45 minutes or until golden brown.

TOPPING

3/4 cup sugar
1/4 cup flour

1/4 teaspoon salt
1 cup heavy cream

Mix the sugar, flour and salt in a bowl. Add the cream gradually, mixing until smooth.

Yield: 6 to 8 servings

Lorraine Miller

CHOCOLATE PECAN PIE

1/2 cup melted butter
1 cup sugar
1 cup light corn syrup
2 tablespoons bourbon
3 eggs, beaten

1/2 cup semisweet chocolate chips
1 cup chopped pecans
1 unbaked (9-inch) pie shell
Whipped cream

Combine the butter, sugar and corn syrup in a bowl and mix until well blended.
Add the bourbon and eggs and mix until smooth. Fold in the chocolate chips and pecans.
Pour into the pie shell. Bake at 350 degrees for 40 minutes. Cool the pie on a
wire rack for several minutes. Serve warm with whipped cream.

Yield: 6 servings

Carole Anderson

A Honey of a Pecan Pie

1/2 cup butter or margarine, softened
1/2 cup sugar
3/4 cup light corn syrup
2 tablespoons honey
3 eggs, beaten
1/2 teaspoon salt

1 to 1 1/2 teaspoons vanilla extract
3/4 to 1 cup chopped pecans
1 unbaked deep-dish pie shell
3/4 to 1 cup pecan halves
Whipped cream
Sherry to taste

Cream the butter and sugar in a large bowl until light and fluffy. Add the corn syrup, honey, eggs, salt and vanilla and mix well. Add the chopped pecans and mix well. Pour into the pie shell. Arrange the pecan halves on top in a decorative pattern. Bake at 350 degrees for 55 minutes. Cool the pie on a wire rack. Serve the pie plain or with whipped cream flavored with sherry.

Yield: 6 to 8 servings

Kathryn Turner

Pumpkin Praline Pie

1 (15-ounce) can pumpkin
1 (14-ounce) can sweetened condensed milk
1 egg, beaten
1/2 teaspoon salt

3/4 teaspoon ground cinnamon
1/2 teaspoon ground nutmeg
1/2 teaspoon ground ginger
1 unbaked (9-inch) pie shell
Praline Topping

Combine the canned pumpkin, condensed milk and egg in a bowl and mix until smooth. Add the salt, cinnamon, nutmeg and ginger and mix well. Pour into the pie shell. Sprinkle with the Praline Topping. Bake at 375 degrees for 40 to 45 minutes or until golden brown. Cool the pie on a wire rack.

Praline Topping

1 cup pie crust mix
1/2 cup packed brown sugar

3/4 cup chopped pecans

Combine the pie crust mix, brown sugar and pecans in a bowl and mix well.

Yield: 8 servings

Jean Gilbert

DESSERTS

*Jose Gaspar's pirate ship
meets its demise.*

JOSE GASPAR:
PIRATE

On May 4, 1904, the Tampa Bay Hotel was
invaded by descendants of the most notorious pirate and krewe
ever to plunder the Florida coast. Or so it appeared until the prominent Tampans
removed their masks and celebrated with their ladies in the hotel's beautiful
banqueting room, thereby initiating the popular "Gasparilla" tradition.
Jose Gaspar, who called himself Gasparilla, was a devil of a fellow.
Handsome of course, tanned, rugged, with $30 million in bounty
to show for a lifetime of thievery and murder on the briny deep.
Once a fine Spanish naval lieutenant, after defeat by the British he had led his compatriots
in mutiny and sailed for Florida. Gaspar headquartered at Charlotte Harbor,
protected by the island he called Gasparilla, by Captiva Island where his captives were held
and by Joseffa Island, named for his mistress. But now at age 65, Gasparilla had decided to bestow
the gold and jewels upon his krewe and lead a righteous life.
Suddenly a British merchant ship appeared on the horizon;
this, then, would be his last capture. As Gasparilla closed in on his final prey,
the disguised vessel pulled down its flag and revealed itself to be the *USS Enterprise*,
its heavy cannon pounding the pirate ship. Knowing all was lost,
Gasparilla cried out that he wanted to die by his own hand and hurled himself
overboard to be devoured by the sea.
Or so goes the legend that has fired nearly a century
of Tampa's colorful sea invasions and parades.

INDIVIDUAL BAKED ALASKAS

1 (8- to 10-ounce) angel food cake
1 quart coffee ice cream, softened
6 egg whites

⅛ teaspoon salt
⅛ teaspoon cream of tartar
¾ cup sugar

Cut the cake into 6 slices about ¾ inch thick. Arrange the cake slices about 4 inches apart on a baking sheet. Spread the ice cream 1 inch thick on the cake slices. Place the cake and ice cream in the freezer. Combine the egg whites and salt in a mixer bowl. Beat the egg whites at high speed until frothy. Add the cream of tartar and beat until stiff but not dry peaks form. Add the sugar gradually, beating constantly until very stiff peaks form. Spread the meringue over the cake and ice cream, covering completely. Place in the freezer until just before serving time. Preheat the oven to 450 degrees. Place the frozen Alaskas in the oven. Bake for 5 minutes or just until the meringue is set and slightly brown. Serve immediately.
Variation: Substitute your own favorite flavor of ice cream for the coffee flavor.

Yield: 6 servings

Lynne Smith

SUNFLOWER DESIGN

England became acquainted with Japanese design when the 1st British Consul in Tokyo displayed his fine collection of Japanese objects at the Great Exhibition of 1851. For many years thereafter, sunflowers copied from Japanese art became a popular motif in English fabric, wallpaper and wrought iron and can be seen on an elaborately carved mantel in the Grand Salon.

DESSERTS

CHOCOLATE CHARLOTTE WITH STRAWBERRIES

28 ladyfingers
Chocolate Layer
2 cups sliced strawberries
2 tablespoons sugar

2 cups heavy cream
1/4 cup sugar
1 teaspoon vanilla extract
Fresh whole strawberries

Split the ladyfingers and line the bottom and side of an English trifle bowl or a springform pan. Reserve the remaining ladyfingers. Pour half the Chocolate Layer into the prepared bowl. Add a layer of the reserved ladyfingers and the remaining Chocolate Layer. Chill until firm. Combine the strawberries with 2 tablespoons sugar in a bowl and mix gently. Spoon over the chilled Chocolate Layer. Cover with plastic wrap and refrigerate until 2 hours before serving. Whip the cream until soft peaks form. Beat in the 1/4 cup sugar and 1 teaspoon vanilla. Spread over the charlotte. Refrigerate until serving time. Garnish with the whole strawberries.

CHOCOLATE LAYER

8 ounces German's sweet chocolate
3 tablespoons water
4 egg yolks

3 tablespoons sugar
4 egg whites
1/2 teaspoon vanilla extract

Combine the chocolate and water in the top of a double boiler over hot water. Heat until the chocolate melts. Beat the egg yolks with the sugar. Add to the chocolate mixture, whisking constantly. Cook over hot water, whisking constantly until the mixture begins to thicken. Remove from the heat and cool. Beat the egg whites until stiff peaks form. Fold into the cooled chocolate mixture. Blend in the vanilla.

Yield: 8 to 10 servings

Sherrill O'Neal

ORANGE CHARLOTTE

1 envelope unflavored gelatin
1/4 cup cold water
3/4 cup sugar
1/4 teaspoon salt
1/2 cup boiling water
1 cup orange juice

2 tablespoons lemon juice
3 egg whites
18 to 24 ladyfingers
2 cups whipped cream (optional)
Orange sections (optional)

Soften the gelatin in cold water for 5 minutes. Mix the sugar and salt in a bowl. Add the boiling water and mix until the sugar dissolves. Add the softened gelatin and mix until completely dissolved. Add the orange and lemon juices and mix well. Chill in the refrigerator until partially set. Beat the egg whites in a mixer bowl until stiff peaks form. Fold the stiffly beaten egg whites into the partially set gelatin mixture gently. Rinse a 1 1/2-quart mold with cold water; do not dry. Line the bottom and side of the mold with ladyfingers. Pour in the orange mixture. Chill until firm. Unmold the charlotte onto a serving plate. Decorate with the whipped cream and orange sections.

Yield: 4 to 6 servings

Kathryn Turner

Lemon Icebox Cake

1 envelope unflavored gelatin
1/2 cup cold water
1 1/2 cups milk
1 1/2 cups sugar
1/8 teaspoon baking soda
6 egg yolks, beaten

Juice and grated rind of
2 1/2 lemons
6 egg whites
18 ladyfingers
Whipped cream
9 to 12 maraschino cherries

Soften the gelatin in the cold water in a large bowl and set aside. Scald the milk in a saucepan and remove from the heat. Add the sugar and baking soda and mix until completely dissolved. Add a small amount of the hot mixture to the beaten egg yolks; stir the egg yolks into the hot mixture. Cook the mixture over medium heat until thickened, stirring constantly. Stir in the lemon juice and rind. Add to the softened gelatin and stir until dissolved. Let stand until cool. Beat the egg whites in a large mixer bowl until stiff peaks form. Fold the stiffly beaten egg whites into the cooled gelatin mixture gently. Line the bottom and sides of a 9x13-inch pan with ladyfingers. Pour in the gelatin mixture. Refrigerate for 24 hours or until firm. Cut into squares and top with a dollop of whipped cream and a cherry.

Variation: Substitute thinly sliced pound cake or angel food cake for the ladyfingers.

Yield: 9 to 12 servings

Clarajo Hurley

Lemon Dessert Soufflé

1 envelope unflavored gelatin
1/4 cup cold water
3 egg yolks, beaten
1/2 cup sugar
1/2 cup fresh lemon juice

1 1/2 teaspoons grated lemon rind
3 egg whites
1/2 cup sugar
1 cup whipping cream, whipped

Sprinkle the gelatin over the cold water in a small bowl. Let stand for several minutes until softened. Combine the egg yolks, 1/2 cup sugar, lemon juice and lemon rind in the top of a double boiler over boiling water. Cook until slightly thickened, stirring constantly. Remove from the heat. Add the softened gelatin and stir until completely dissolved. Pour the mixture into a large bowl. Let stand until cool but not set. Beat the egg whites in a bowl until stiff peaks form. Beat in the remaining 1/2 cup sugar gradually until very stiff peaks form. Fold the egg whites into the lemon mixture gently. Fold in the whipped cream. Pour the mixture into a decorative 6-cup mold or into individual molds. Chill or freeze overnight. Unmold the soufflé onto a serving plate. Garnish with additional whipped cream, fresh strawberries or chocolate sprinkles .

Yield: 8 to 10 servings

Wilma Martin

The de Soto Oak

In the 1500s, the Spanish explorer Hernando de Soto sat in the shade of an oak tree and made peace with the Timucua Indians. The live oak has aged into a giant of a tree, spreading its branches beside what is now Plant Hall's Grand Entry. There are those who question the veracity of this tradition, for history has not treated de Soto kindly. But the legend, if such it be, is certain to endure, given that myths are often more admirable than harsh reality.

MY FAVORITE CHEESECAKE

6 eggs
1 1/2 cups sugar
1/2 teaspoon salt
1/2 teaspoon vanilla extract
Juice of 1 lemon

48 ounces cream cheese, softened
Crumb Crust
Cherry pie filling or fresh
strawberries (optional)

Combine the eggs, sugar, salt, vanilla and lemon juice in a medium bowl and beat at low speed until thick and lemon-colored. Beat the cream cheese in a large bowl until creamy. Add the egg mixture and beat until smooth and creamy. Pour into the Crumb Crust in the prepared springform pan. Bake at 350 degrees for 1 hour or until set. Broil for several seconds to brown lightly if desired. Place on a wire rack to cool. Refrigerate until thoroughly chilled. Loosen the cheesecake from the side of the pan. Remove the side of the pan and place the springform base on a serving plate. Serve plain or topped with cherry pie filling or fresh strawberries.
Variation: Blend 2 cups sour cream with 1/4 cup sugar and pour over the warm cheesecake. Sprinkle with 1/2 cup graham cracker crumbs. Bake for 5 minutes and cool; chill as above before serving.

CRUMB CRUST

1/2 cup Zwieback or graham
cracker crumbs
3 tablespoons sugar

1/4 teaspoon cinnamon
1 egg white

Combine the crumbs, sugar, cinnamon and egg white in a small bowl. Press over the bottom and side of a greased 10-inch springform pan.

Yield: 16 to 20 servings

Francine Dobkin

CHEESECAKE IN A PIE PLATE

16 ounces cream cheese, softened
3 eggs
1/2 teaspoon vanilla extract
2/3 cup sugar

2 cups sour cream
1/3 cup sugar
1/2 teaspoon vanilla extract

Combine the cream cheese, eggs, 1/2 teaspoon vanilla and 2/3 cup sugar in a mixer bowl and beat for 5 minutes or until very smooth and creamy. Pour the mixture into a well greased 10-inch pie plate. Bake at 325 degrees for 50 minutes or until set. Cool on a wire rack for 20 minutes; the filling may fall slightly while cooling. Combine the sour cream, 1/3 cup sugar and 1/2 teaspoon vanilla in a small bowl and blend well. Pour the mixture over the partially cooled filling. Bake at 325 degrees for 15 minutes. Let stand until completely cooled. Chill in the refrigerator.
Variation: Substitute almond extract for vanilla in the cream cheese mixture and garnish the cheese with slivered Brazil nuts just before serving.

Yield: 8 servings

Helene Straske, Ivy Hollingsworth

JOE, THE ONE-EYED ALLIGATOR

When the city of Tampa acquired the old hotel and grounds in 1905, little did it realize that it had bought itself a zoo. At first there were just a peacock, a monkey who answered to the name Dan, and Joe, the one-eyed alligator. Then a big black bear joined the motley crew, to the delight of the children whose families arranged Sunday afternoon excursions to the Plant gardens. But Joe was snapping at the furry new arrival, and Dan had taken to sulking and throwing banana peels into the bear cage. Clearly it was time for the city to move the wildlife off to larger quarters.

CHOCOLATE VELVET CREAM

8 ounces cream cheese, softened

¹/₄ cup sugar

1 teaspoon vanilla extract

2 egg yolks, beaten

1 cup chocolate chips, melted

2 egg whites

¹/₄ cup sugar

1 cup heavy cream

³/₄ cup chopped pecans

Chocolate Crumb Crust

Whipped cream

Combine the cream cheese, ¹/₄ cup sugar and vanilla in a mixer bowl and beat until well blended. Add the egg yolks and melted chocolate and blend well. Beat the egg whites in a mixer bowl until soft peaks form. Add ¹/₄ cup sugar gradually, beating until stiff peaks form. Fold the stiffly beaten egg whites into the chocolate mixture gently. Whip 1 cup cream until soft peaks form. Fold the whipped cream into the chocolate mixture gently. Fold in the pecans. Pour the mixture into the Chocolate Crumb Crust. Freeze until firm. Loosen the Chocolate Velvet Cream from the side of the pan and remove the side. Decorate with whipped cream and serve immediately.

CHOCOLATE CRUMB CRUST

1¹/₂ cups finely crushed chocolate wafers

¹/₃ cup melted margarine

Combine the crumbs and margarine in a bowl and mix well. Press over the bottom of a 9-inch springform pan. Bake at 325 degrees for 10 minutes. Let stand until completely cooled.

Yield: 12 servings

Anita Gillen

PUMPKIN DESSERT

1 (29-ounce) can pumpkin
1 (12-ounce) can evaporated milk
3 eggs
1 cup sugar
1/2 teaspoon salt
2 teaspoons ground cinnamon

1/2 teaspoon ground ginger
1/4 teaspoon ground cloves
1 (2-layer) package yellow cake mix
1 cup chopped nuts
3/4 cup melted butter

Combine the pumpkin, evaporated milk, eggs, sugar, salt and spices in a large bowl and mix well. Pour into a 9x13-inch baking pan sprayed with nonstick cooking spray. Sprinkle the cake mix evenly over the pumpkin mixture. Sprinkle the nuts over the cake mix. Drizzle the melted butter over the top. Bake at 350 degrees for 1 hour or until golden brown. Serve with whipped cream, whipped topping or ice cream.

Yield: 16 servings

Sylvia Frazier

Poached Pears with Grand Marnier Sauce

4 medium pears	Fresh mint sprigs (optional)
3 cups water	Raspberries (optional)
1 cup sugar	Melted chocolate (optional)
Grand Marnier Sauce	

Peel the pears, leaving the stems intact. Core the pears carefully from the bottom end. Bring 3 cups water and 1 cup sugar to a boil in a medium saucepan. Place the pears in the saucepan, reduce the heat to a simmer and cover the saucepan. Simmer for 20 minutes or until the pears are tender. Remove the saucepan from the heat and let the pears cool in the poaching liquid. Remove pears from the poaching liquid and drain well. Spoon a small amount of the Grand Marnier Sauce onto dessert plates. Place a pear on each plate. Decorate with mint, raspberries and melted chocolate.

Yield: 4 servings

Grand Marnier Sauce

2 egg yolks, beaten	2 tablespoons Grand Marnier
1/4 cup sugar	1/2 cup whipping cream,
2 tablespoons water	whipped

Combine the egg yolks, sugar and water in the top of a double boiler and beat until well blended. Cook over gently simmering water until very thick and fluffy, beating constantly with an electric mixer at medium speed. Pour the sauce into a small bowl. Stir in the Grand Marnier. Let cool for 10 minutes. Fold the whipped cream into the mixture.

Yield: 1 cup

Sherrill O'Neal

STRAWBERRIES MARSALA

3 pints fresh strawberries
1 1/2 cups sugar
2 cups water

1 (3-inch) cinnamon stick
1 (1/4x1-inch) strip lemon rind
Marsala to taste

Rinse the strawberries and remove the caps. Pat the strawberries dry, place in a large bowl and set aside. Combine the sugar, water, cinnamon and lemon rind in a saucepan. Bring to a boil, stirring until the sugar dissolves completely. Remove from the heat and add the Marsala. Let stand until cool. Discard the cinnamon and lemon rind. Pour the syrup over the berries. Chill until serving time.

Yield: 8 servings

Nootchie Smith

REGAL CHOCOLATE SAUCE

This recipe has been a favorite in the Tampa area since 1961.

1/2 cup light corn syrup
1 cup sugar
1 cup water
1 teaspoon vanilla extract

3 (1-ounce) squares unsweetened
chocolate
1 cup evaporated milk

Bring the corn syrup, sugar and water to a boil in a heavy saucepan, stirring until the sugar dissolves. Cook to 235 degrees on a candy thermometer. Remove from the heat. Stir in the vanilla and chocolate. Stir in the evaporated milk gradually. Store, covered, in the refrigerator.

Yield: 3 cups

Lynn Carlton

ANGEL BAVARIAN

An excellent light choice for a ladies' luncheon.

1 1/2 envelopes unflavored gelatin	4 egg whites
1/3 cup cold water	2 cups whipping cream
2 cups milk	Cream sherry to taste
1 cup sugar	1 angel food cake
4 egg yolks	2 cups whipping cream
2 tablespoons (heaping) flour	Red food coloring (optional)
1/8 teaspoon salt	Shredded coconut

Soften the gelatin in the cold water. Combine the milk, sugar, egg yolks, flour and salt in a saucepan and mix well. Bring to a boil, stirring constantly and remove from the heat; the custard will be thin. Add the softened gelatin and stir until completely dissolved. Let stand until cool. Beat the egg whites in a mixer bowl until stiff peaks form. Whip 2 cups whipping cream. Fold the sherry, stiffly beaten egg whites and the whipped cream into the custard. Tear the cake into pieces and place in a large tube pan. Pour the custard into the cake pan, allowing it to flow around the cake pieces. Chill, covered, in the refrigerator overnight. Loosen from the side of the pan. Invert onto a serving plate. Whip the remaining whipping cream and tint pink with food coloring if desired. Frost with the whipped cream and sprinkle with coconut.

Variation: Substitute 2 packages of whipped topping mix prepared using the package directions for the whipped cream.

Yield: 10 to 12 servings

Lynn Carlton

Chocolate Pots de Crème

1 cup semisweet chocolate chips
2 tablespoons sugar
1/8 teaspoon salt
1 egg
1 teaspoon vanilla extract

1 1/2 to 2 teaspoons dark Jamaican rum
or 1 teaspoon instant coffee powder
3/4 cup milk, scalded
Whipped cream

Combine the chocolate chips, sugar, salt, egg, vanilla and rum in a blender container and process lightly. Add the hot milk. Process for 1 minute or until smooth. Pour into ramekins. Chill for 1 hour or longer. Top with whipped cream.

Yield: 4 servings

Lynne Smith

Tampa and Early Flight

On a frosty winter morning in 1903, the Wright brothers managed to keep their hand-built airplane aloft for an incredible 12 seconds. Man had been given wings and the courageous of the world dared to design, test and perfect marvelous new flying machines. For a decade, commercial application of the airplane consisted of the occasional joy ride in an open cockpit until, in America, a scheduled airline service began covering the 20 long miles between St. Petersburg and Tampa, Florida. A young man named Tony Janus had the honor of piloting the single-passenger flying boat. In Roman times the God of Beginnings was called Janus, hence our name for the month of January. Tony Janus appears to have been aptly named: he made history with this "aviation first" on January 1st, 1914.

White Chocolate Mousse

This was a specialty of the old Harry K's restaurant.

12 ounces white chocolate   5 egg whites
³/4 cup unsalted butter   ¹/3 cup sugar
5 egg yolks

Melt the chocolate in a double boiler over hot water or in a microwave-safe bowl in the microwave. Melt the butter in a separate container. Combine the melted chocolate and melted butter in a large mixer bowl and blend well. Add the egg yolks 1 at a time, beating well after each addition. Beat for 5 to 10 minutes or until thick and creamy. Place the egg whites in a copper bowl if available. Beat the egg whites until soft peaks form. Add the sugar 1 tablespoon at time, beating until stiff glossy peaks form. Add half the stiffly beaten egg whites to the white chocolate mixture and mix just until blended. Fold in the remaining egg whites gently. Spoon into a serving bowl and chill or freeze for several hours to overnight. Serve the mousse with a garnish of dark chocolate curls or leaves and/or nap the dessert plates with chocolate sauce before adding the mousse.

Yield: 10 servings

Anita Gillen

Coffee Chiffon

2 tablespoons unflavored gelatin
1/2 cup coffee liqueur
3/4 cup sugar
3 cups strong hot coffee

1 cup whipping cream
1/2 teaspoon salt
1 tablespoon vanilla extract

Soften the gelatin in the liqueur in a large bowl. Add the sugar and hot coffee and
stir until the gelatin and sugar are completely dissolved. Chill until the mixture is almost firm.
Beat until the mixture is light and fluffy. Combine the whipping cream, salt and vanilla
in a bowl and beat until soft peaks form. Fold the whipped cream into the gelatin mixture. Spoon
into a glass serving bowl or individual stemed glasses. Garnish with shaved chocolate
or chocolate coffee bean candy. Chill in the refrigerator until serving time.
Variation: Substitute fat-free topping for the whipped cream for a truly forgiving dessert.

Yield: 6 to 8 servings

Nootchie Smith

Founder

*Henry Plant knew a good deal when he saw it and he had the gumption
to act on his convictions. It was a kind of wisdom to be sure, but not the
scholarly kind; Henry never had been one for book learning. He was a man of
action with pioneering instincts, a calm and courteous gentleman whose
imperishable confidence in the South gave Tampa its soul.*

Spanish Caramel Custard

Most chefs only use six eggs but I have never tasted a flan
anywhere that is more delicious! This recipe has been
in my husband's family for 50 years.

6 1/2 tablespoons sugar

4 cups milk

1/2 teaspoon salt

1 sliver of lemon rind

1 cinnamon stick

1 1/2 cups sugar

1 teaspoon vanilla extract

10 egg yolks

2 whole eggs

Cook the 6 1/2 tablespoons sugar in a small skillet over low heat until a golden
caramel color, stirring constantly. Divide the caramel among 10 to 12 custard cups, tilting the
cups to coat the bottoms. Set the cups aside. Combine the milk, salt, lemon rind and
cinnamon stick in a saucepan. Heat the mixture until scalding and set aside. Combine the
1 1/2 cups sugar, vanilla, egg yolks and eggs in a bowl and beat with a wire whisk while counting
slowly to 25; the mixture should be light and fluffy. Whisk the milk mixture into
the egg mixture. Strain the mixture into the prepared custard cups. Place the filled custard cups
in a large shallow baking pan with hot water. Place the pan in a 300-degree oven. Bake for
1 hour or until the custard is set. If bubbles appear in the water, add a small amount of cool water;
the water should be hot but not boiling. Remove the custards from the hot water and
let stand until cool. Chill in the refrigerator until serving time. Loosen the custards from
the sides of the cups and invert into dessert dishes.

Yield: 10 to 12 servings

Sharon Smith

PUMPKIN CUSTARD

3 eggs
3/4 cup canned pumpkin
1/2 cup maple syrup
2 tablespoons brown sugar
1/2 teaspoon ground cinnamon
1/4 teaspoon freshly ground nutmeg

1/2 teaspoon salt
2 cups milk, scalded
1 teaspoon vanilla extract
3 ounces cream cheese, softened
1 tablespoon (about) milk
Chopped pecans

Beat the eggs slightly in a large bowl. Add the pumpkin, maple syrup, brown sugar, cinnamon, nutmeg and salt and blend well. Add 2 cups milk and vanilla gradually, beating constantly until smooth and creamy. Spoon the custard into 6 custard cups. Place the cups in a shallow baking pan with 1/2 inch hot water. Bake at 325 degrees for 45 minutes or until the custards are set. Remove from the hot water and let stand until cool. Beat the cream cheese with a small amount of milk to make a topping of light and fluffy consistency. Top each custard with a dollop of the whipped cream cheese and sprinkle with pecans. Serve the custards at room temperature or chill before serving if desired.

Yield: 6 servings

The Late Sylvia Vega, Charter Member

Sticky Toffee Pudding

¹/4 cup sugar

¹/4 cup butter, softened

1 egg

1¹/2 cups flour

1 tablespoon baking powder

1¹/4 cups chopped pitted dates

1¹/3 cups boiling water

2 teaspoons instant espresso powder
or instant coffee powder

1 teaspoon vanilla extract

1 teaspoon baking soda

Brown Sugar Sauce

Combine the sugar, butter and egg in a large mixer bowl and beat for 2 minutes. Sift the flour and baking powder together. Add to the creamed mixture and beat for 1 minute. Combine the dates, boiling water, espresso powder, vanilla and baking soda in a bowl and mix well. Add to the flour mixture and beat until well mixed but do not overbeat. Divide among 6 or 8 greased 3/4-cup custard cups. Place the cups on a baking sheet. Bake at 350 degrees for 30 minutes or until a wooden pick inserted in the centers comes out clean. Place the cups on a wire rack to cool. Loosen the puddings from the sides of the cups and invert onto dessert plates. Serve with warm Brown Sugar Sauce.

Yield: 6 to 8 servings

Brown Sugar Sauce

²/3 cup packed brown sugar

3 tablespoons unsalted butter

2 tablespoons whipping cream

Combine the brown sugar, butter and cream in a small heavy saucepan. Bring to a simmer, stirring constantly until the brown sugar dissolves. Simmer for 3 minutes, stirring occasionally.

Yield: 3/4 cup

Helen Chavez, The Tea Room in Old Hyde Park

Tiramisù

8 egg yolks, at room temperature
10 tablespoons sugar
¼ cup sweet marsala
¼ cup brandy
1 pound mascarpone cheese
2 cups whipping cream, whipped
1 cup strong espresso, cooled

2 tablespoons sweet marsala
2 tablespoons brandy
16 to 20 ladyfingers
2 ounces bittersweet chocolate, grated
Baking cocoa to taste
Cinnamon to taste

Combine the egg yolks and sugar in a mixer bowl and beat until thick and lemon-colored. Add ¼ cup marsala and ¼ cup brandy and beat until blended. Add the mascarpone and beat until smooth. Fold in the whipped cream gently. Mix the espresso with 2 tablespoons marsala and 2 tablespoons brandy in a shallow dish. Dip each ladyfinger in the espresso mixture and arrange half the ladyfingers to line a 9x13-inch dish. Pour half the whipped cream mixture into the prepared dish. Sprinkle with the grated chocolate. Repeat the layers with the remaining ladyfingers and whipped cream mixture. Garnish with a generous sifting of the baking cocoa. Add a sprinkle of cinnamon. Chill, covered, for 6 hours to overnight or freeze if desired. Mascarpone cheese can be purchased at an Italian market.

Variation: Egg substitute can be used in place of the egg yolks.

Yield: 8 to 10 servings

Pat Gillen

Cookbook Committee

CO-CHAIRS

Beverly Rogers   Lynne Smith

COMMITTEE

Cookie Bailey   Lorraine Miller
Lynn Carlton   Mary Pope
Helen Davis   Pat Schiff
Diane Kemker   Elaine Watson
Phyllis Kimbel   Robbie Williams

Recipe Testers

Carole Anderson
Beverly Austin
Cookie Bailey
Joanne Baldy
Monk Brannan
Helen Brown
Susan Bulger
Annlynn Byrd
Lynn Carlton
Dot Cason

Patsy Clifford
Pat Colvard
Ann Crowder
Helen Davis
Betty Farrior
Joanne Frazier
Sylvia Frazier
Anita Gillen
Pat Gillen
Emalou Grable
Nibia Griffin

Jane Hewit
Clarajo Hurley
Phyllis Kimbel
Carole King
Pat Martin
Joan McKay
Bertha Nelson
Lib Nelson
Mary Pope
Mary Baker Robbins
Judy Rodriguez

Sarah Jane Rubio
Susie Sanders
Pat Schiff
Nancy Segall
Barbara Skyrms
Ruth Turbeville
Kathryn Turner
Martha Ward
Mary Wolfe
Betty Wood

CONTRIBUTORS

Beverly Anderson
Carole Anderson
Mary Anderson
Beth Arthur
Beverly Austin
Patty Ayala
Cookie Bailey
Joanne Baldy
Laura Bentley
Monk Brannan
Eloise Brooker
Sally Brorein
Anne Robbins Butler
Lynn Carlton
Jane Carswell
Dot Cason
Helen Chavez
Marge Christopher
Patsy Clifford
Ann Cloar
Marjorie Cochran
Pat Colvard
Dot Compton

Ann Crowder
Betty Culbreath
Pat Culbreath
Beth Darr
Helen Davis
Margaret Davis
Marsha Dickey
Libby Dickinson
Alice Dingle
Francine Dobkin
Freddie Ennis
Betty Farrior
Mary Lee Farrior
Martha Ferman
Bertha Fletcher
Joanne Frazier
Sylvia Frazier
Cynthia Gandee
Mary Ellen Germany
Mary Jean Gibson
Jean Gilbert
Anita Gillen
Pat Gillen

Emalou Grable
Nibia Griffin
Martha Hall
Mia Hardcastle
Doris Harvey
Pene Herman
Jane Hewit
Marte Hill
Nadyne Hines
Mary Ruth Hodges
Ivy Hollingsworth
Mark Holmberg
Sallie Holmberg
Sue House
Lora Hulse
Clarajo Hurley
Vicki Hussey
Taylor Ikin
Mary Anne Ingram
Louise Jackson
Nell Lee Keen
Diane Kemker
Phyllis Kimbel

Carole King
Elaine Litschgi
Charlotte Logan
Helen Martin
Pat Martin
Wilma Martin
Carol Mathews
Joan McKay
Ellen McLean
Ruthanne McLean
Patsy McNichols
Camille McWhirter
Lorraine Miller
Judy More
Holli Morris
Lenda Naimoli
Bertha Nelson
Elaine Newman
Jackie O'Conner
Sherrill O'Neal
Bob Paige
Dada Pittman

Josephine Pizzo
Sharon Pizzo
Mary Pope
Mary Baker Robbins
Judy Rodriguez
Beverly Rogers
Nell Rorebeck
Sarah Jane Rubio
Adajean Samson
Susie Sanders
Pat Schiff
Nancy Segall
Ginger Tarr Shea
Barbara Skyrms
Lynne Smith
Nootchie Smith
Olliff Smith
Pat Smith
Sharon Smith
Paul Sparks
Barbara Starkey
Margery Starns

Sara Charles Stevens
Helene Straske
Vera Swirbul
Ann Thompson
Dot Trigg
Ruth Turbeville
Kathryn Turner
Martha Turner
Sylvia Vega
Sarah Wahl
Martha Ward
Charla Wash
Elaine Watson
Jane Watson
Connie West
Pat Wilson
Betty Wood
Patsy Woodroffe
Marion Wooten
Gwen Young
Sarah Zewadski

INDEX

Spinach Roulage in Puff
Pastry, 160
Spinach Sandwiches, 20
Spinach Soufflé, 159
Spinach Soup, 65
Spinach-Stuffed Tomatoes, 161

SQUASH
Butternut Squash Casserole, 165
Retreat Squash Casserole, 166
Squash and Apples, 164
Squash Casserole, 164

TOMATO
Asparagus and Tomato
Bundles, 143
Dried Tomatoes, 162

Green Tomato Bake, 152
Spinach-Stuffed Tomatoes, 161
Tasty Tomato Pie, 139
Tomatoes Rockefeller, 136
Yum-Yum Tomatoes, 137

TURKEY
Marinated Turkey, 103
Santa Fe Soup, 58

VEGETABLES. *See also* Individual
Kinds
Carrot Soufflé, 145
Cauliflower Soufflé, 146
Celery Casserole, 147
Eggplant Quesadillas, 119
Hearty Cabbage and Bean Soup, 57

Hopping John, 153
Polish Bigos, 83
Ratatouille Provençale, 163
Senator Russell's Sweet
Potatoes, 167
Vegetable Pie, 138

WILD RICE
Chicken and Wild Rice
Casserole, 98
Florida Wild Rice, 73
Wild Rice and Oyster
Casserole, 111
Wild Rice Party Dish, 71
Wild Rice with Olives, 72

Victorian Secrets
The Chiselers, Inc.
P.O. Box 14494
Tampa, Florida 33690-4494

Phone orders may be placed by calling (813) 926-8251.

Please send _____ copies of *Victorian Secrets* .... $24.95 each $ _____

Plus postage and shipping .... $ 4.00 each $ _____

Florida residents add sales tax .... $ 1.75 each $ _____

Total $ _____

Please charge my [ ] VISA [ ] MasterCard   Account Number _____

Expiration Date _____ Signature _____

Name _____

Address _____

City _____ State _____ Zip _____

Make checks payable to The Chiselers, Inc.

Photocopies Accepted